Developmental Coaching

Books by Martin Shervington

Peak Performance through NLP
(with John Seymour)
Don't think of Purple Spotted Oranges!
Developmental Coaching
The Celebrity Coach
The Quan
Life: you can't stop the waves but you can learn how to
surf
(with John Seymour)
Professor Winston's 'Human' – contributory author
Successful Manager's Handbook – contributory author

Developmental Coaching

A personal development programme for professionals, executives and coaches

Martin Shervington

British Library Cataloguing in Publication Data.

A catalogue record for this book is available from the British Library.

ISBNs Paperback 9781780921808
ePub 9781780921815
PDF 9781780921822

MX Publishing, 335 Princess Park Manor, Royal Drive, London, N11 3GX.
www.mxpublishing.co.uk
Cover Design by www.staunch.com

This book is dedicated to Tim Healey for his enormous support, direction and encouragement when first writing and studying in this area; John Seymour for his kindness and friendship, as well as for writing the preface; Brian van der Horst for his friendship over the years; Gavin Hall and John and Jenny Gower for being there when I needed you most; and my Mum and sister, Sally, for all their support throughout my life.

Contents

Preface by John Seymour

I have, over my life, seen coaching develop from simply sports coaching, to become the second biggest form of consultancy, after management consultancy, with many specialisations such as executive coaching, life coaching, etc. I have also witnessed, over the last ten years, a proliferation of coaching books. I notice that the skills of NLP have had an increasingly influential role in the development of coaching itself. I welcome the development of coaching and believe it plays an important part in helping individuals cope, and even thrive, in a world of explosive complexification.

In teaching NLP, I have found that when I outline the stages of consciousness, as mapped by Ken Wilber, Clare Graves and others, it gets a lot of 'aha's, particularly from coaches. This happens when I explain how the coaching varies with the developmental stage of the person you are working with.

Martin's book is particularly timely for the world of coaching. It is not often that a book can change the nature of a discipline. By showing how the nature of problems changes with the different defences typically used at the different stages of development of consciousness, this book can change how we think of coaching.
I have known Martin for many years, so I know his depth of fascination with the stages of consciousness. He practices what he preaches to an unusual degree and is a particularly good guide to the different developmental stages of consciousness. Reading this book saves a lot of time and effort over reading the original sources and Martin has done an excellent job of simplifying the complex and making it readily available.

As far as I know, this is the first coaching book to focus so clearly on the different major stages of consciousness, the defences/adaptations/pathologies of each stage, and how to work with them as a coach. It deserves a place in the library of every practicing coach and anyone interested in the main stages of personal development.

8

Introduction

Competence and consciousness

30 years ago, if you asked people to think about coaching, many would have associated the concept with a middle-aged man, wearing a sports shirt better suited on a teenager but who, nonetheless delighted in improving his baseball or football team's performance. Not so many years on, things have changed beyond recognition. The term "coach" has found its way into newspapers, magazines, boardrooms and performance reviews. Coaching has become a process for improving an individual's behavioural performance in such wide circles - it continues to go from strength to strength. Whether it is executive or life coaching, many people already have a coach, are a coach or would want a coach if they knew where to look. Coaching is on the up.

There is certainly a market for coaching in business, as well as in more general life situations. I know many coaches that are very well paid – £450 an hour (about $650) for executive level coaching. This may not be you "thing", but be assured there are many people that would be delighted with a good coaching session for nearer £100 ($150). With coaching becoming one of the fastest growing career moves for people looking for an alternative employment route, there is certainly sustained energy in the field. US News and World report states '...the profession of...personal coaching...is the second biggest consulting business, second only to management consulting.' The Washington Post agrees '....in the next few years, coaching will become the norm in the business world.' Fortune Magazine adds 'Done right, coaching clearly works.'

Having worked in the area of personal development for over 15 years now, I have seen coaching become a support structure for some, and a way of achieving better results for others. In my own coaching experience, however, I have built up an approach with over 100 clients that delivers something a little different. Developmental Coaching, as I have called it, is an edu-coaching method whereby I coach people but also explain in detail the models or principles I am working with. What I have found has surprised me - people really come out of the coaching process a "different person". Not everyone, but so many of my clients have found the developmental framework we work with transforms their lives. This really does work.

Many years ago I wrote an e-book called Integral Coaching thinking this was the process I was taking people through. Having had so much experience since that time, I have adapted, flexed and changed what I do into "Developmental Coaching". It is not totally "integral" as some people would see it and I am quite happy with that. It does have, however, several integral models that I've found useful. I had seen many a glazed look at the attempted explanation of many a theoretical model; you learn not to use some things that are best left in books. Through one-to-one experience I have distilled what I thought was important for people to learn and experience into what actually works for them.

My aim of this book, for you the reader, is to take away a solid theoretical framework that can be used to enhance coaching sessions. Even if you are not a coach you will still be able to apply all of the principles in any case. In fact, every professional, manager and executive will gain some useful insights into how they are put together. I will talk in terms of a 'coach and a coachee' throughout but you may well be taking on the role of both, at least initially.

The aim throughout is to a) give you a model, b) give you points of application and then c) let the pieces build up into a developmental view of a person. As you will see, Developmental coaching is not "flat" once you get into the flow of it all. There are certain shifts in consciousness that can be supported through this approach, all the time considering the person you have in front of you and what they are looking to achieve. If you were to look for a coaching a unique coaching approach, it would be Developmenal Coaching's strong focus on psychological development whilst understanding everyone's hangups that are stopping them achieving their dreams. I present it with my own preferred models, helping me to slice and dice what it means to be human. In this way, this book brings together several authors' work and will offer insight into how to take coaching to further depths. It is, however, the 'Adaptations' session that I feel you won't find elsewhere.

Integral Psychology

This book, then, is based on the work of many authors, including the work of Ken Wilber and Robert Kegan (primarily for consciousness evolution), George Vaillant (adaptive mechanisms),

Carl Rogers (client-centred therapy) and Howard Gardner (Multiple Intelligences). What I have tried to do with each of these authors' work is abstract a few key aspects that I have found useful for coaching sessions. There is far more I could include (and some would say "should" if it was to be truly "Integral") but I have decided that this book is going to be an authentic expression of what I have found works. That's it folks. I am not attempting to give you a full spectrum developmental experience all the way through to enlightenment; nor am I going to talk about personality types and tell a story of when INTJ, ISTJ, INFJ and ENTJ walked into a pub (reference Myers Briggs, for those who don't know it). The truth is, I don't use that in my coaching sessions. What I use most of the time, and what has worked for me, is contained in this book. That is all.

There is an Integral Psychology influence throughout as I find that to be very handy to run through with clients. As such, it is worth explaining that a little more.

Integral Psychology emerged relatively recently through the work of Ken Wilber. It was and is a way of making sense of all the different schools of psychology and philosophy. They all were looking at 'life', reaching their own conclusions and then considered their view as either always 'right' or 'whole'. Small battles would often then occur to hold onto their bit of territory. Wilber, as a master map maker, pieced together that there *was* sense somewhere within it all – that there were ways of looking at life that respected many schools of psychology and philosophies. As such, Integral Psychology is not so much a new school of psychology, but a way of looking 'over and beyond' disparate viewpoints.

Personally, I love this stuff! I originally began exploring what was probably hundreds of books, finding myself and being cerebrally invigorated along the way. It has been the point of application of one-to-one sessions with clients that has moved it out of my head and into my body. I know for some people, theoretical models are about as dull as a rainy afternoon, but if I can excite you just a little I hope to explain how useful this will be in your life, as well as with any clients you may have. This "stuff" transforms lives.

So, where did I get my guidance from when I got started with all of this, I hear you cry? Well over many years I have been fortunate enough to have several adept coaches and mentors. This is the reason I began studying this area so ferociously. I did a Law and Business Degree when I was a mere slip of a lad before doing my post grad studies in Organisational Psychology a little later on. It was through extra-curricular studies for years during and afterwards that I started to 'get it'. I have, of course, applied everything I am writing about to a great extent in my own personal development. Still learning, still reading, still working on it all, but I do 'get it'.

I have been lucky in this respect for sure. The coaches I have had personally have pushed me to places I couldn't have known existed and my passion for exploring my mind and my world still burns inside.

So, if you are a coach looking to extend your abilities, I would encourage you to have an open mind to this approach. If you are looking for a theoretical framework you can apply to your own life then you are in luck as well. At the end of each chapter I aim to give you areas of application. This enables you to "hang" the theory onto some real life hooks. I've structured the book as seven sessions in an attempt to show you how all of the information can be used with a client. You are free to do what you want, juggling content around sessions if it works best for you both.

Before we get on a roll, we should consider coaching as having two potential aims. The first relates to performance enhancement of competencies. We will be considering this, of course, but it is not part of our main content as many coaching books already focus on this. This approach to coaching is usually primarily interested in the person learning to 'swing the racket' or 'perform the task' better. The second is interested intimately with the person who is doing the 'swinging'. This is where the real "development" comes in.

Fundamental principles

I mentioned earlier Developmental Coaching is coaching with a twist. Well, maybe more like a spiral. It may well address issues, concerns, problems or goals at the current level of consciousness but it will also support the individual to review and reflect on the process as well. It is through this objectification and model building that people disembed from their previous structure of consciousness (how they view the world; the "I" that they were becomes a felt sense of someone "different") into a place, as one client said to me, that "just works better". In this respect, this is about helping another individual evolve or develop through a process of *transformation*.

In his book *Flatland*, Reverend Abbott beautifully illustrates what could be considered as a movement between levels. The story begins with a square who fell asleep and has a dream. "Square" dreamt he had fallen from Flatland, the land of two dimensions (where he was a square) into Lineland, the land of one dimension, where he had become a line. This was a transformation, but in a backwards direction and a rather disturbing one too. In this land there are no squares, circles or hexagons, just lines. The little square had lost his sides – and was feeling very lost indeed. What made it harder in this dream was his inability to explain to the King of Lines (who ruled this land) that he was not a line, but a square. Eventually the Linelanders turned on him but he managed to wake up before they caught him. Back in Flatland where Square was comfortable, his sides having returned to him once more, he was teaching mathematics to his grandson (who happened to be a hexagon). The little hexagon was learning algebra – about three long and three wide – when he asked if there was anything more than three by three?

The grandfather (Square) scoffed at the thought that there could be a dimension more than the flatland in which they lived and told the hexagon not to trouble himself. But when little hexagon had gone home, Square said out loud, 'The boy is a fool, I say'. As he said these words, a sphere appeared and announced its presence. Sphere, from the third dimension, only appeared as a wobbly shape that would come and come (because, in Flatland, Square could not see the third dimension). The story continues with Sphere taking Square on a journey into the third dimension – an expansion of being for Square as he became a cube.

The story ends with Square becoming so enthused about his new consciousness that he starts wondering if there is anything beyond that. He asks Sphere about the mysteries of dimensions beyond Sphereland, at which point Sphere says, 'There's no such land. The very idea of it is inconceivable,' and then throws him back into Flatland where Square ends his days trying to convince people of this third dimension. Sadly, in Flatland, he is not believed.

This story is a beautiful illustration of shifts upwards and downwards, of perspectives and limits. In this story, you can also see a concept of "translation" - such as learning more of the same mathematical problems better (on a level), but this is not transformation. Transformation is when the learner is radically transformed through the process of learning and actually develops. They "take a leap" as the maths moves from the second to the third dimension.

This is, one of our aims with Developmental Coaching. I am certain many other coaches out there are doing this; I just want to give people a few models that will help in the process. It is through these, Developmental Coaching may well differentiate from other forms of coaching.

In Flatland (and any other land), however, there is a reluctance to accept there is anything beyond – something for ourselves, and as a coach we all need to avoid, if we want to assist in transformation. I will not, however, be looking beyond the "normal" transformations one tends to experience within the culture of coaching. As such I will simply allow the reader to look at Wilber et al for guidance in areas of a more transpersonal nature and focus on what I think will be useful to hear from me instead. I have both passion and interest in that area but I have would rather focus on what I have found with 95% of clients. I may have taught some basic meditation techniques, discussed the nature of mind and even joked about the cosmic game, but I believe this book will be most useful to you if I spend time considering other forces.

Competence considered
One of the aims of coaching, in more general terms, is to aid improvements of performance. So, before we kick off with the way to approach coaching sessions themselves, let us consider

16

competence. This will get us "on the same page", so to speak, when it comes to coaching and how it can be a method for improving many a skill. It is skills that we will now focus on, in particular what needs to be in place "within" a person in order for a skill to stick.

A coach will help a person get a result, improve a metric, or perform to a higher standard. As such, it is the desire to increase competency (either verbally, or in action, or both) that is the starting point for most coaching. This area of competence (skill) enhancement needs to be seen as considerably important. In fact, despite focusing more on the transformational framework within this book, it would be remiss of me not to recognise how essential it is to increase competencies as well. In the overall picture we can place competency actions largely *within* a level. And it is only when that competency has become sufficient that the possibility of a movement to a higher level occurs. My aim then, is to bring together the importance of both the moves *within* levels and the moves *between* levels.

So, now looking further at an individual's performance, Competence Considered by Sternberg and Kolligian, is a collection of psychologists' essays considering the importance of our own perception of performance and how this will in fact affect performance itself. In their essay, Markus, Cross and Wurf explore this issue. It has become increasingly common that people consider that 'imagery and mental practices for future attainments prepares one for the actual performance'. This alone, often as a mental rehearsal technique, can aid in attaining a level of skill. In its' simplest form this might be imagining every small step of a task successfully being achieved, playing out every detail so our neural networks are all fired up and ready to go. As consciousness is embodied, there will be an affect on the body itself – there will be micro muscle movements and sensations when the individual imagines performing the future scenario. This has significant consequences for everyone's performance and is already widely known in the world of sports, presentations and management tasks. The technique is one of mentally performing an event in preparation for the actual event, being used to improve the end result.

In the same context, there is also the question of self-image, e.g. 'I am a good learner', and this can be semi-permanent and most often beyond awareness. It is the internalisation of a self-image (words and/or images) that has a profound role in our achievements. The self system (the "place" where all this "lives") contains the self-images. But it is when the images are capable of holding the person back, e.g. 'I am bad at maths', it is likely that this will be the end result, i.e. the person will be bad at maths. It is only when an individual creates a 'possible self' in the future that is 'good at maths' that they can become orientated towards attaining the goal in the future. 'When one has a sense of competence, one *will be competent* (or be on the way to becoming competent), or at least relative to one's self without this feeling.' This feeling of being competent is a vital and integral component of competence. As the adage goes, if you think you can, or you think you can't, you are probably right.

Competence may *either* develop from a person having a particular ability and then build a kind of self structure around it, or from a person developing a self-structure and then using it to motivate the acquisition of the actual ability. In other words, they have either got it, or they need to be motivated enough to develop it. It is when our perceptions of ourselves are negative that we have already begun to set course for a lower level of achievement. Tootlkits (including Neuro-linguistic programming, NLP) are very handy in this area. For instance, someone may shift their emotional state, alter internal self-image and set goals, all of which help the person move towards their desired state. It is the movement towards a future 'possible self' that generates even more motivation and increases the likelihood of action.

The culture that an individual operates within also affects their level of competency. When a skill is valued by a community, e.g. a child's skills of singing being valued within their family, it is more likely that, over time, the individual will take on board the views that other people have of them and their skill. Small amount of positive reinforcement will make a big difference. It is a bit like someone having their own "like" button (reference to facebook) that can be pressed when other members want to reinforce the behaviour. Often it is subtle, but if this is consistent over time, an internal self-image will be constructed that supports that view. Similarly, if the child is able to develop the skill further within their social system, e.g. attending a specialist music/drama school, again their performance can be changed further (as well as their self-image). But if the culture or 'social environment fails to support them, or the requisite skills fail to develop, many of the possible [future] selves may be abandoned.' Over a long period, a person will find it hard work to maintain the self-image without the necessary skills that the image supports.

Albert Bandura says, 'It seems that most skills develop only when the opportunity exists. Thus unless somebody believes a person can develop certain skills, such hidden potential may never exist.' Through coaching, the individual can be encouraged; and through this encouragement they can construct a self-image that supports and motivates them to attain the level of skill that the coach may see as a potential emergent quality. I bet you've heard this yourself. Someone who "knows" sees the potential in a colleague, a junior football team, a music teacher and so on. It is not just the belief that they can achieve the goal that is important, it is also their 'representation of *herself* or *himself* approaching and realising the outcome.' So the person needs to be experiencing change toward the goal, not just having a belief they are "great". That can be easily taken away when someone fails at one too many sales calls, lets a 'goal in' or turns out to play the violin like strangling a cat. Bandura continues, 'when faced with difficulties, people who have self-doubts about their capabilities slacken their efforts or abort their attempts prematurely and settle for mediocre solutions, whereas those who have a strong belief in their capabilities exert greater effort to master the challenge.' It is often not actual capability that is the critical and determining factor; it is the belief about that capability that makes all the difference. For instance, when two people are compared, one may perform better in social environments. In actuality their competence in the environment may be equal, but their self-image is the driving force in the difference in performance. They see themselves as a great networker or the life and soul of the party. When performing a task then, actual ability is important, but self-perception is crucial. When an individual has the necessary self-perception of capability they are more likely to search out solutions and become creative in their attempts. They will bounce back from any failures more

19

quickly when the self-structure is oriented in a more positive fashion. 'Because the acquisition of knowledge and competencies usually requires sustained effort in the face of difficulties, it is the resiliency of self-belief that counts.' Bandura continues 'self-doubts produce substantial increases in subjective distress and psychological arousal.'

I bet you are wondering how you can use this principle? Well, for the coach, this is of vital importance. It is through that relationship of coach and coachee (or client, or friend, or colleauge, I may well interchange these words dependant upon the formality of the coaching) that a change can occur and result in differences in performance, whether it is in a sport, relational or career context. As Bandura explains, 'Self-limitation of career development arises more from perceived self-inefficacy [negative self image] than from actual inability. By constricting choice behaviour that can cultivate interests and competencies, self-disbeliefs create their own validations.' So, let us flip this around: if you, as a coach, support someone to build a positive self image then you are part way their to them moving toward their goals. This is the emotional element within a coaching context, you can really talk people into believing they can do it. This is the concept of the self-fulfilling prophecy.

I began this section by saying that competency articulation is fundamentally important both in coaching, as in life, for an individual to acquire and perform at a skill. In the coach's role, encouragement is essential because helping to maximise existing or potential competencies will allow other stages to emerge. But the starting point will always be the development of skills from their current position. This is what you have to work with.

The end of translations
Moving on from the increase in skills now, it is time to explore the way an individual can not only move within a level (becoming more skilful) but how they can move between levels (and transform who they are). This is probably a slightly different view on coaching but is nonetheless important for Developmental Coaching.

Failure is a concept that general coaching tends to shy away from, but within Developmental Coaching it is an essential ingredient for the individual taking a leap, i.e. only when all their translations (options) fail can there be a transformation. This is when everything the coachee has done (this is what I mean by failure in this context) has proven to be *unsatisfactory*, irrespective of whether the actions were 'successful' or 'unsuccessful'. It is this un-satisfactoriness (yes, made up word) that is the foundation needed for a transformation opportunity to occur. If the translations continue to work, then the coachee will be 'content' to keep continuing with them – transformation will only occur when the coachee is dissatisfied, or 'discontent' with the translations at their existing level. You will have come across this many times- people fail so they stop trying. Instead, an example would be when someone is no longer content with an unsatisfactory relationship and instead finds a way of transforming it. For instance, this could be done by asking of oneself and the other party to the relationship 'What is the nature of relationship you would like to have?' This is one of my favourite questions to ask in relation to any relationship. If all you take away from this book is this sentence then I will be delighted. It is very handy. As Paul Watzlawick says in 'The Pragmatics of Human Communication', this disembeds the individual from the dynamic of the old relationship and comments about the relationship itself. In fact this questioning of oneself initially allows for an outcome as to the desired nature of relationship. Without this it is very common that the relationship would continue with the usual translations such as arguments, silence, irritation etc. It is when these translations have failed e.g. you get fed up of arguing, that the possibility of transformation can occur. The end point of this type of process (the asking about the nature of relationship) is not inevitable, but it creates the opportunity of fundamentally altering the relationship. It creates the space for transformation.

Here we have started to look at the "context" of the relationship, not just the "content". So often we get caught up in the content- they did this, they said that- and we fail to look at the relational context. It is an illuminating prospect to reflect on situations in this fashion.

To 'move on' a level you need discontentment with the state of affairs at the current level. Without it, the move to another level will not have the necessary energy for it to emerge. As we can also see in a business content, any progress needs to come from being discontent. Small shifts and changes in a business to keep it on track are translations. So often when a new leader emerges or joins a company they will change the path the organisation follows and set a path for transformation. Psychologist Dr Clare Graves sees that this is somewhat par for the course: 'At each stage of human existence... man is off on his quest to find his holy grail, the way of life he seeks by which to live... He believes he will find the answer to his existence. Yet, much to his surprise and much to his dismay, he finds at every stage that the solution to existence is not the solution he has come to find. Every stage he reaches leaves him disconcerted and perplexed. It is simply that as he solves one set of human problems he finds a new set in their place. The quest he finds is never ending." Ok, not the most upbeat and cheerful of quotes, but at each stage there is hope. This hope comes in the form of ongoing transformation to higher and higher levels. This overcomes the dissatisfaction inherent within explored and conquered ways of being and knowing. This is where Developmental Coaching can really come in. Yet the coach cannot rush the process – they cannot rush in and force a transformation upon someone – it will occur if and when the conditions are right. The coach should support the coachee in exploring and implementing suitable interventions at the existing level of consciousness, such as helping them increase their competencies. You might even find that these interventions are what the coachee will stick with for a very long time. If the coachee has a long cycle of remaining content prior to the experience of dissatisfaction, the coach must simply allow the coachee to sit in that contentment. After all, this is about the coachee's life, and well-being, in as large a context as possible. Even if transformation never occurs, this is fine. Afterall it is not your marriage, your business, your life, even though you may care.

It is more likely, however, that the translations will prove at some point to lose their appeal, and as soon as contentment ends, the cycle will naturally return to the coachee seeking new satisfaction. We have all had this experience ourselves. This is when we desire, for example, a new car or new clothes and once we have them we find that they do not fulfil us any more. So off we go, in search of a new translation that may satisfy for another period of time. It is only when all the translations are unsatisfactory that the coachee will become incarnated with the opportunity to transform.

Transformation

Transformation is the natural process for the emergence of a new way of being and has already occurred several times within all of our lives. Let us begin with explaining one reason why this is so important at this time. Currently many people are finding that the present way of understanding is simply inadequate for the complexity of life. We have to balance partnerships with parental interests; children with work; work and free time; intimate relationships with friends, and so on. Life has reached an increased level of complexity through changes in economic, technological and social areas and it is evident just as much in the battle in the cultural domain about differing perspectives of the 'correct' worldview. Most often though, what hasn't changed is the way we think about what we think. This is different to the content of the thoughts, the images and words – this is about our *way of thinking*. A more complex life requires a more complex level of thinking. Without this more complex level of thinking, people may feel like a fish out of water. When anyone feels like this, they truly feel stranded and without the support (internally) to engage in life in an appropriate manner. It may all sound a little extreme, but this is nothing new and has happened to us before. It may have been the first day of school for a four-year-old, the first sexual experience of adolescence, or the first day of work in a corporate structure. The feeling is one of being out of our depth – or to continue the analogy – without the depth of water that gives us security. It is not that the person could have prepared more; nor could they have expectations of their new environment. Instead, the person is experiencing something that requires a new level of making meaning of their reality. And it is not to say that the meaning-maker will find the transition either quick or easy. What they will find though, is that in order to fit into the new mode of being – including the increased expectations that are made of them – there has to be a radical change in the way they think. It is not just how a person behaves, nor is it what they think – it is about *how they think*. The person's consciousness (mind) itself requires a radical readjustment and expansion in order to tackle a new level of complexity.

This is no longer about competencies; this is about consciousness. The fish, as it were, needs to learn how to fly. This is a different sort of coaching as well.

Keeping it real
On a final note for this Introduction, although this approach encompasses all aspects of being human, you will be pleased to hear it does not need the coach to be expert in all the content of the world. It is similar to a sailor who has expertly navigated his ship through many oceans. He knows about the ocean with its many characteristic waves, but that does not mean he is an expert on how to paddle a canoe, as this is quite different to sailing. The coach is able to understand the background, the ocean, but should remain authentic to his or her area of expertise, sailing. We all have different levels of competency in many different areas; we need not specialise to be most forms of coach but we do need to see that the coach's authenticity within a specific field is likely to be a binding factor within the coaching relationship. If this was later to be shown as inauthentic, the coaching relationship would fail. For example, a coach who has never been in a long-term relationship would not be authentic to talk about one at depth. They could, however, coach the person in a less interventionist way about looking at what they wanted to be different in the long term relationship. The coach is then able to assess the various elements at play within the individual that could assist or restrict the direction decided upon. There are often stories of holy men who have behaved in ways contrary to their teachings, it is very much like that. The congregation are rarely forgiving.

This leads me to questions 'who is a coach?', 'who is not a coach?', 'who is a teacher?' or 'who is a mentor?' Well, I will answer it simply: I am not a purist. For deep Developmental Coaching there will need to be sustained contact over time, but I am suggesting that anyone who comes in contact with another can be a coach – this could be a five-minute conversation in the street that helps another individual to shift into a better frame of mind. The skills and models you will learn in the rest of this book will be useful in many situations. Simply use them as you choose and try your best to enjoy the interactions. As I mentioned earlier, it will also be great for your own personal development. The more you enjoy the person, the better a coach you will be.

24

With all of this in mind, let us now start looking at the content of the sessions and getting some of the skills and models on board.

Session 1

Goals and your coaching relationship

Getting started - goals and your coaching relationship

Thinking long and hard as to how best give you this approach to coaching, I have broken the book into seven main sessions. This is what I have typically covered with numerous clients over the years. There is, of course, a little juggling here and there if needs be; the aim is all about the coachee so remember to put them first instead of trying to follow a formula. I guess this is why my approach could be a little different now to 10 years ago. I know the content inside out and realise the key factors needing to be delivered as and when.

A coaching frame

So, although many Developmental Coaching sessions will never follow such a rigid structure, it is useful for us to think through the practical application of an existing and well-known coaching process, i.e. Tim Gallwey's GROW model. This model is current currency for personal and professional development and provides us with a starting point within the existing practice of many coaches. For those unfamilar, Gallwey's 'GROW' model, that I have adapted slightly, has four main stages:
G – Goal
R – Reality
O – Options
W – What next?

This model works enormously well because much coaching has historically been behaviourally based and we will be looking at individual's behaviour within cultural and social system contexts a little later on. At the start of a session I will usually just let the coachee/client chat away as I build up a decent picture of "where they are at". Everything l I have ever learned will be leaping in my mind, from NLP, to developmental psychology, to Ekman's work around micro-expressions, as they are chatting away. The reason I think in terms of GROW is to find out where they are, where they want to be (if they know) and what is stopping them getting there. But it may be very complex when one lifts beneath the fragile veil as the relationship starts to develop. GROW, gives us a little normality that helps people build trust we are listening to what they are saying. Let's give a broader overview of GROW to kick us off:

Goal

In life there are three main places we can be – moving forwards, moving backwards or standing still. Maybe it is inherent within human nature that moving forwards somehow 'feels' better than the other two options – certainly it does over a long period. When we feel we are moving on, we are orientating ourselves to something that is important to us, and it is such orientations that we call goals. Without goals there is a tendency to drift or stagnate. Goals allow our mental energy to have a consistent and focused channel – without them, our mental energy tends to dissipate. Mihaly Csikszentmihalyi, in his book Finding Flow says: 'intentions focus psychic energy in the short term, whereas goals tend to be more long term and eventually it is the goals that we pursue that will shape and determine the self that we are to become.... Without a consistent set of goals, it is difficult to develop a coherent self. It is through patterned investment of psychic [or, mental] energy provided by goals that one creates order in experience.'

Goals then, are more than just striving for personal achievement – they are able to bind the psyche. This binding process will tend to hold a person together as a consistent 'goal orientated' individual instead of feeling 'in pieces'. But it is interesting how this ties in with William James's view that self-esteem depends on the ratio of expectation to successes. Csikszentmihalyi says, 'A person may develop low self-esteem either because he sets his goals too high, or because he achieves too few successes'. The goals we set, then, are important.

In the realm of goals it is healthy to focus on what you want from life (or any smaller aspect of it). When you focus all your time on what you don't want, you tend to expend much mental energy on the very things you don't want. It is the process of exploring exactly what you do want that many people find a challenge – luckily it does get easier with time.

As the coach, you should encourage the coachee to be specific about their desired goals. If you then find the coachee's body language and voice tone is unconvincing, i.e. they are uncertain about their desired goals, you may even decide to ask 'Is that what you really want?' Such incongruence will tend to make the whole

GROW process fall apart unless you pick up on it – but it will not mean that the coaching process itself totally falls apart. Really, setting goals in a session is really almost an excuse in itself for the coach and coachee to transform themselves through their relationship. Whether the goals are achieved very quickly or not, whether the goals change over time and whether the coachee is happy to achieve and move on, will all depend on how the coachee is put together as an individual within their life circumstances. There are no golden rules – although goals will allow the relationship to have the semblance of a normal coaching relationship while focusing the coachee's internal balance and helping them move on.

It is worth mentioning that in personal relationships, the coach should support the coachee's goals, not what the coach wants. In this way, it is ideal to have moved through the realms of development oneself as the coaching process becomes 'cleaner' as to self and other interest.

In the traditional behavioural types of coaching, 'reality' is easy to understand, e.g. if the coachee wants to delegate more effectively, then the coach will usually identify that they currently 'feel' bad about delegating, and that their results are never as good as they want. From this state it is quite simple to move to the next stage, i.e. looking at what the coachee could be doing differently. It will be a behavioural change through the coachee asking the person they are delegating to to repeat back precisely what the coachee asked them to do. And this may suffice in many coaching sessions. Not wanting to overcomplicate things (but wanting to make things suitably complex), the individual at this 'reality' stage is often not looking at the factors that underpin their behaviours in order to understand why they are getting the unwanted results. Instead, in a conventional coaching mode, the coachee is looking primarily at things they can do differently. There may be a shift in the 'feel' aspect to some extent, but I am suggesting that this will not be a transformational leap. If the coachee is able to point at the problems within themselves (and use of the appropriate language can actually lead to some liberation from the symptoms) and say, 'Ah...this is happening because....' (low affect, low interpersonal line of development, high level of narcissism etc), they will be able to choose to develop accordingly. It is through understanding oneself and one's foibles that we can liberate ourselves from our negative traits. The coach is the support function, the mirror and the fountain of authentic knowledge from their life experience who will aid this 'reality' process.

If a deeper restructuring does not occur, the coachee will encounter a problem at the 'same level' at some point in the future. It may have nothing to do with delegation, but it will have the same flavour as the underpinnings of the initial coaching 'reality' stage. On the other hand, transformation leads to liberation from a problem at the same level.

Options

In much conventional coaching, and taking the example of a challenge in communication with another, the coach would ask the coachee to come up with options to solve their own problem. And in conventional coaching, this is the based on the principle that the coachee must solve the problem and it is more than likely that they have the resources within themselves to do so. Developmental Coaching does not believe the second of these points. Many of the resources are simply not available to us. For instance, we have all had experiences of strong negative emotions – when we are hit by this level of emotion, our normal resources simply are not present. Also, Developmental Coaching sees that the process of 'problem solving' is an imperative part of development. It is through the process of problem solving that transformation has the opportunity to occur. As the problem solved is an integral problem (not just behavioural), it is also likely that a simple behavioural change will not change the factors that underpin the problem (though the surface problem may well shift). Developmental Coaching requires an almost constant effort of individual development to move beyond the level where the current problem is being experienced – it will be then that the problem is looked at with different eyes.

So, the options that are explored are both at the current level – a shorter term fix – and at the higher level whereby the individual has transformed themselves and the relationship they have to a problem. The coach's role is to support the coachee as they explore and try out the solutions at the initial level. Over time, and with understanding, the coachee will often find that these 'translations' fail. The answer they are looking for requires not a 'shift' but a 'leap'. When all the 'shifts' fail to satisfy, a leap can occur. However, shifts are an essential part of the process as well.

What next?
This is often seen as the 'wrap up' section of a coaching session. As there is usually some further action to be undertaken, there is usually a 'what next?' The coach often knows that at the 'what next?' stage, the most suitable potential options will have already been narrowed down at the previous stage. Now it is simply a case of deciding what to do next and when. This initial 'next step' is often more than solving the more behaviourally oriented problem (as in the case, for instance, of delegation mentioned earlier). But there will also be support toward a developmental step that will be a leap. This may be through the suggestion of reading material (if the coachee is open to such an approach) or through setting up a 'check in' coaching meeting or call. This second meeting or call takes the theme of the GROW session a little further. Through the constant effort of the coachee and the support of the coach, the coachee will resolve the more fundamental issue over time – or that is the ideal.

I have brought Tim Gallwey's GROW model throughout the explanation above whilst beginning to explain a little more about the concept of transformation as well. Now I want to give a sample of how this can be applied within the wider Developmental Coaching framework, so we will look at the areas of Health, Business and Relationships.

Health
In the health arena, the repression of health issues (or even denial) can be a way of dealing with them in the short to medium term. We can probably all relate to this whether it is back pain, aching knees or getting short of breath. Often we push aside minor ailments that we can 'live with'. It seems as though we can accept a certain amount of background pain in our lives and even though this level of tolerance is personal, something can happen that makes the level 'too much'.
This is the ideal time for the Developmental Coach to appear on the scene, i.e. when the threshold of tolerance has been reached or maybe even exceeded. When this occurs, the previous route of ignoring or denying the problem has not worked and something

now needs to be done. The coach's role is to establish what the individual wants (Goal), what is currently happening (Reality), what are the options (Options) and then what they will do next (What next?). In reality it is never quite this simple or straightforward, but it is a starting point.

With health issues, the coach needs to tread very cautiously as, presuming good health themselves, they need to be appreciative of the coachee's feelings more than ever. State of health, and specific health issues in particular, extend into our sense of self – who we are. To become unwell can often undermine the feelings we have about who we are and this in turn can cause secondary problems – 'Not only am I unwell, but I am also feeling 'bad' about being unwell.' The coach's role is, again, one of support. In particular, if the coach can support the coachee emotionally by listening to the 'reality' of the problem first (instead of rushing into the 'goal'), the coachee will feel more validated as an individual. The goal is presumed to be a moving away from the current state of ill health and into one of better health. This probably does not have to be spoken to be understood.

Once the person feels validated, it is likely that their emotional state will shift to a slightly more positive one (at least in the coach's presence). This is when the coachee will feel more able to explore the options they have – this may well be further exploration of medical options, research, conversations with understanding fellow subjects who have the condition etc.

The coach will have been thinking through the areas of health that are present within physiology, mind (both are usually thought of as 'health'), relationships and, let's say, money (as both relationships and money have an impact on health). Also, the individual with their defences and levels of development will be considered.

As the above shows, while the coachee has applied the GROW model, they have done so in a kindly fashion that is appreciative, understanding and tolerant of the coachee and their situation. Let's now look at a few examples to explain how this can be used even more.

Business

In the context of business, the GROW model is well known and well used. One coach I know spends much time asking 'what if?' oriented questions when they come to the 'options' stage of

GROW. This is useful to get people who are stuck in patterns of responses to explore possibilities further. It is quite usual for a coach to look at desired goals (e.g. outcomes in a monthly breakdown of a business plan) and the current state of affairs in that context. What is often more crucial is thinking through the implications of the coachee's actions, or 'what if?' It is this 'what if?' thinking that broadens the coachee's horizons in the system within which they are operating. For instance, if the coachee is involved in a change process, such as a new computer system, it is not just the system changes that need to be appropriately dealt with – the coach may also point out, 'So, if you do that, what will happen?', prompting the coachee to explore the consequences (both positive and negative). The coachee may then think through how their team will feel about this – maybe a higher degree of inclusion within the change process could help these cultural relations. There might also be specific job role alterations that need to be looked at before, during and after the change, e.g. 'who will be responsible for this?' There may also be attitudes and beliefs among the coachee and their colleagues that need consideration – such as 'is it all worthwhile'? The more bases the coachee can cover, the more likely the change process will produce the desired results.

The above explanation of 'what if?' thinking still operates within a closed system, whereby the variables are said to be 'known', but of course this is rarely the case. It is when 'what if?' thinking is extended to its furthest reaches that something else begins to emerge. The coach can help the coachee explore the options and expand the remit within which these options are explored. However, it is primarily the coachee's own role within business and their level of thinking and being that determines the direction of exploration and, often, the results obtained.

Relationships
I am unsure whether it is just my own idiosyncrasy or more general, but I am reluctant to systematically work through the GROW model within the context of relationships. By their very nature, relationships are not one sided and as I mentioned earlier, maybe the ideal relationship is one where we are changed through the process of relating.

35

I think that to examine GROW within the relationship context requires the relationship to have a context too, so let us use the example of a family dispute to illustrate the use of GROW in the loosest terms. Let's face it, we've all been there! It is quite possible within this context that the coach can facilitate the coachee gaining a perspective that allows them to have a 'relationship with the relationship'. If a young person has a relational dispute with a parent, they may find themselves permanently frustrated in their parent's presence. As the problem is probably not a new one, it could be that the coachee has insufficient personal resources to deal with it. Quite simply, any 'move' they make is at least matched by the parent – after all, within that relationship, the parent has many more years' experience of playing relational games. Without choosing to enter relational theory here but rather to look at the coachee themselves, we can see that being better at playing the game will only benefit one party – the parent. If this is the case, the relationship itself will not improve; the balance will just slowly shift in direction. What can be done instead is to release the coachee from the habituated patterns (games) through development. So in a coaching session, we may begin with the goal that 'I want a better relationship with my parent' and then the current frustrations are explained. The coach can then help the coachee, maybe for a time, to fail as often as they possibly can. It is through this failure within the relationship (i.e. the failure of the 'game') that the coachee reaches the edge of available possibilities – they run out of gaming options, and even not playing is part of the game. It is at this point that the coachee may well transform and begin to see what it was about their dependence and embeddedness within that relationship that was holding the relational problem in place. When they glimpse from the outside that this is the case, they have transformed. They are now able to have a relationship to their relationship with the parent.

When the coachee then relates to the parent in future, there will be a difference. It is not a coldness because of the distance, but rather putting the relationship in perspective to see the form that it used to be. In turn, the coachee will feel differently as they see their own role within the dynamics that led to the initial relational challenge. Interestingly, the affect on the coach as they 'hold' the coachee through the process is one to be greatly appreciated. The coach can do little within the actual exchanges, but throughout them the coach's role is often internalised (in the form of words or images) during the exchanges. The coachee has taken on board not just the information of the coach, but also the flavour of the coach's approach as it lingers in their mind as they talk within that relational context. They will feel supported.

By using the models in this book, you can bring order to your relational exchanges – no matter the length. But the coachee and the coach's relationship with them should be the overriding concern, not just 'getting a good result'.

The coaching relationship
Generally in coaching, people speak of the coaching contract – an explicit (maybe even a written) agreement about the roles and responsibilities of both the coach and the coachee. The coaching contract sets the participant's boundaries and expectations for the relationship. If you are going to do it, it is likely to be set up in this session, Session 1.

This leads us nicely onto the nature of relationship you are seeking to have with your coachees. Coaching within the personal development and business context is generally seen as taking a non-interventionist approach – the coachee brings a problem to the session and the coach pulls out the resources within the individual to solve it. The coach does not generally offer solutions or nudge the coachee in any particular direction. While I fully respect this approach, Developmental Coaching is rather different in that it is only non-interventionist up to a point. When an individual is showing signs of a particular challenge (or use of a certain immature adaptive stance), the coach may well suggest a route that will encourage the coachee to develop in this area. Interestingly, this may be uncomfortable for the coachee at the time as there is usually an unconscious aversion to following such a route. That the coachee nonetheless accepts the discomfort is based on the relationship that is developing between themselves and their coach. As coaching is not therapy, the contract allows the coach to explain from the outset that the relationship is one of support for the coachee – not therapy. This is an important point in relation to the potentially high level of intervention in Developmental Coaching. When appropriate, the coach offers unobtrusive guidance – but guidance it remains. The coach is able to see many patterns of behaviours the coachee eludes in the coaching session, and depending on their competency, the coach will begin to build a map of the individual. This map will include the coachee's adaptations, lines of development and level of consciousness etc. Their role will then become similar to the therapist in one sense – they won't 'therapise', but they will 'hold' the individual. As therapist Carl Rogers said: *'If I can provide a certain type of relationship, the other person will discover within themselves the capacity to use the relationship for growth, and change and personal development will occur.'*

This 'holding' is one of the fundamental aspects of Developmental Coaching. The support function is not that of a crutch to be leaned on, but of a receptive container that pours forth compassion and understanding, receiving in return the pleasure of observing another individual's growth and development. The function of holding will, however, increase in effectiveness when the coach understands 'how to hold' what is 'to be held'. There is a difference between holding of the vase and holding the long stemmed rose. This book will help you understand how to hold and appreciate more what is being held.

I remember talking with a Tibetan lama who told me that lamas need to appreciate and enjoy their student's neuroses – in this sense, how the student increases the suffering in their life. Similarly the Developmental Coach must appreciate and enjoy the coachee's present personality level while at the same time supporting the emergence of their next level. I believe the coach's level of enjoyment is a crucial factor. It is this enjoyment that inspires the coachee to explore their options while feeling 'held'. Anyone who knows me realises I like people. I get excited and enthused around them as I enjoy exploring their world. I also truly enjoy seeing them develop. As Rogers said in his book *On Becoming a Person*: *'This book is about me...as I rejoice at the privilege of being a midwife to a new personality – as I stand with awe at the emergence of a self, a person, as I see the birth process in which I have had an important and facilitating part.'* As Rogers sees it, it is important for there to be three conditions necessary for this type of relationship: 'being genuine', 'accepting' and 'understanding'. So, what does this mean for you as a coach at the start of this new relationship?

'Being genuine' - This means 'I need to be aware of my own feelings...rather than presenting an outward facade of ones' attitude, while actually holding another attitude at a deeper or unconscious level.' This may not be a simple task but, as Rogers explains: 'it is only by providing the genuine reality within me, that the other person can successfully seek for the reality in him. I have found this to be true even when the attitudes I feel are not attitudes with which I am pleased, or attitudes which seem conducive to a good relationship. It seems extremely important to be real.'

'Accepting' means 'a respect for liking him or her [the coachee] as a separate person, a willingness for him to possess his own feelings in his own way. It means an acceptance of and a regard for his attitudes of the moment, no matter how negative or positive, no matter how much they may contradict other attitudes he has held in the past.'

'Understanding' means a deep understanding of their [the coachee's] world as if seeing it through their eyes. The thoughts and feelings the coachee may have can be seen as they see them and then accept what is seen. 'There is a freedom from any moral...evaluation.'

I stress again that Developmental Coaching is not the same as therapy. What it *is,* is a relationship between two people that irrevocably changes the people themselves. This is what I have found in so many of the coaching relationships I have experienced.

When a car is driven down a road, we often think that it is the car that is acting upon the road. This is a view of a one way relationship and may be analogous to a teacher who continues to teach in the same way irrespective of the student he or she is teaching. If however, we see that the car is actually being irrevocably affected by the road as well, we see a two way relationship. As the car may drive down the road everyday and hit the same potholes, the car itself begins to become affected. The tyres may become more worn and the suspension may become increasingly shocked. Again and in turn, the car may affect the potholes on the road as it drives into them – they deepen and broaden with every journey. This is the same as the relationship between coach and coachee – it affects them both and cannot be a one way thing.

To be coach or a coachee and not be deeply touched over time by the experience means you were probably never engaged in the relationship in the first place. The same goes for all other relationships as well. When I said you need to 'appreciate and enjoy' the coachee, I meant this wholeheartedly. You need to embrace the relationship with such zeal that you too are bound to develop in the process. Every interaction will create an experience that both people will reflect upon. After the initial reflection, the coach in particular will adjust their internalised model of the world so that the next meeting with *any* coachee will follow a different path to the one had the interaction had not been experienced. It is this testing out that leads to a new experience in the latest interaction. This in turn feeds the coach during their reflective times, leading to yet another internal adjustment. It is this continuous process that allows the coach to develop to higher and higher levels of expertise. Throughout this cycle, the coach is going through a process of internal adjustment that could well lead to their own development. If this occurs, it is a transformational process. Using the car as a metaphor again, the road itself may have been restructured and resurfaced – and the coachee (as we will talk about much more) may find that their transformation comes through a radical replacement with a new development of the design of, let's say, the suspension units. Potentially this can be a dialectical process whereby the selves within the interaction are transformed by the interaction itself, illustrating the developmental attribute of Developmental Coaching for both parties. As my coach has said to me, 'this is not one sided.'

Aside from the prerequisite that the coach needs to really like the coachee, there is the fact that you can't coach everyone you come in touch with in the same way or to the same depth. Even though the Developmental Coaching approach can filter into a one-off five-minute conversation at the local shop, this is not to the depth that is required for the coach to have the long-term affect. It is the longer relationships that lead to far greater potential of transformation of one's circumstances and oneself than the alternative. So, with a longer-term view, the coach must be aware of their level of commitment to the potential coachee from the start. This is imperative as the level of attention given during the 'holding' process can be so high that to remove it suddenly could harm to the coachee. It would probably be better not to coach them at all if this was likely to occur. Instead, the coach must make a rational decision about whether they have the time, competence and patience to support the development of another other human, i.e. the coachee.

Past experience tells me that there will be a string of people who would appreciate your support and understanding. If you decide to enter into several orienting conversations with a potential coachee, it is highly likely that a coaching relationship will develop – whether you call it that or not.

As the relationship develops and continues through the sessions you may recognise you have a mentoring relationship as a coaching one with some people. The coachee may be able to gleam knowledge from you that is far beyond 'pulling information'. After all, suggestions can often be very useful. Differently to a non-interventionist approach to coaching, if someone has a vast well of experience and wisdom, a loving approach and is oriented towards justice, then it seems a shame not to drink from the fountain of advice once in a while. For instance, taking my personal passion for writing, if I personally was only coached in the behavioural sense by my own coach, I may have focused on how 'I could write shorter more sentences for greater impact'. Instead I was able to develop *through* my writing because my coach's interest was not in the standard or structure of my first books, but rather how I could develop to write at higher and higher levels. Both approaches are important within coaching, but quite different in nature. This is why, for Developmental Coaching purposes, I choose not to differentiate between 'coaching' and 'mentoring' too much because the relational aspects of this approach transcend but include both practices. I will leave it to you to decide where to draw the line.

So, to wrap up this first section, let us look at a few case studies of actual people I have coached in this way.

To begin, in one coaching case with a family member, Anne, she would never have called herself a coachee (which is probably a good thing as the relationship is the important element, not the codification) but nonetheless, she was coached towards a deep understanding and a suitable intervention for a health issue.

Anne was on a waiting list for publicly funded treatment of a knee complaint. The initial consultation had produced a diagnosis that surgery was appropriate – however, the complaint was not considered urgent (according to the criteria of the system) and she was placed on a two year waiting list. One year passed with the usual contact on weekends. The coachee had waited patiently, but the waiting had taken its toll – the condition had worsened and her quality of life had begun to drop dramatically. The impact of not being able to use the limb to any more than 25% capacity had begun to affect her emotionally and also impacted on those around her. The coach, me, with a gentle approach listened as a friend, instead of being an outcome focused relative. Sometimes, with family more than anyone, we really need to let them talk. All her needs were understood and her unhappiness and discontentment with the system were acknowledged. She felt supported despite the condition remaining the same. But it is not this that led to a breakthrough – it just 'held' her long enough to allow what happened next. I've experienced waiting lists for operations (and knew 'the system'), and was able to loosen Anne's thinking around what was happening. Anne felt it was her place to 'wait' and not try to 'queue jump'; when the coach pointed out the fallibility in her thinking – that in this case the system in reality did not process cases in the way she believed – Anne was able to see through what had previously held her back. She decided not to wait any longer, but demanded a new appointment with a consultant. Following the coach's advice, Anne approached the consultant in a different way. Instead of feeling the consultant was 'above her', she engaged the consultant in a more human fashion – talking as she would talk to a respected friend – an approach he found refreshing. This gentle push led to an operation within four months; it also began to increase her proactiveness to explore the financial compensation within the benefits system for those unable to work due to disability.

The coach, in this case me, operated in a fashion that encouraged Anne to 'get over' the internal concerns of approaching the consultant once again, and this led to an improvement in her physical and emotional well being. The exchanges also showed that the relationship with the consultant, within the context of the system they operated, could be adjusted to the benefit of them both.

Anne, by the way, is my wonderful and very brave Mum.

In another case, I recall being very cautious about giving explicit conventional advice to a potentially great young manager and leader I was asked, by him, to coach. Especially as the basis to this coaching situation was more about appreciating how to help a young manager to become a true leader by learning and developing *within* their role, *through* their role and *beyond* their role, making it was unnecessary to understand the ins and outs of their daily activities. Instead, the I spent some time supporting the manager to objectively view how the changes they were asked to instigate would affect all the members of the business. This process integrated many more variables, including a deep estimation of people's responses to new changes and challenges they would face as their department began to grow. From there the coachee was able to take action with fresh insight.

This is an example of how the approach was about helping the coachee to operate at a level of thinking and being that was suitable of the complexity faced. My job was not to help with the task side of the coachee's work, but to focus on developing the person who was thinking and being. The coachee was delighted with the level of personal support, but it came out of many years of a relationship that has required honesty on his part as well. I am still in touch with this manager who has since taken a promotion and doubled his salary since the time he was employed. As it happens, he was one of my employees when I ran a training business and a good chap to boot.

Relationship and relational issues can also have a broad range – from personal and intimate issues through to business relationships can be seen within the coaching context. These are sometimes the most difficult areas of our lives to open up, but the rewards of a caring and understanding 'ear' can transform the individual. In the simplest of cases, the coach may act as a mirror to the individual's own actions that reflects them in a light that had not previously been seen. We all have blind spots – the coach may well give us the eyes to see. To give another example, the coach may simply 'hold' the coachee when they feel the pain of a relational breakdown. This was my best option in a coaching situation that came simply from a phone call from an old client. This holding can be the temporary support structure that, even though the pain still remains, gives hope that it will one day end. Something in the relationship with the coach leads to an increased understanding that this is part of life and, as with all things, will pass. It is the ability to talk through with utmost confidence and discretion that can be the difference between loneliness and inclusion within a culture. This is something to be cherished within the coaching relationship. So as we end this section, you will have a flavour of the role of the coach and, hopefully, some ideas on how to approach a Developmental Coaching session.

Questions for reflection:
Will you use a structure to your coaching sessions?
What are the strengths and limitations of a structured approach?
What other skills will you bring to the session?
What boundaries will you define, eg: timescales? content matter?
Is this about setting a goal or changing the person playing the game?
What kind of relationship do you want with your coachees?

Session 2

Lines of development

Lines of development

As a coach you will come across a broad range of people with mixed abilities in many different areas of life. Because all these coachees have different interests, types/levels of ability and different areas of application, this session will explore how you can encourage the emergence of their unique qualities. This is about the individual and where they want to 'go' (or 'grow') and, maybe, where they could go if only they had the eyes to see. It is through the coach/coachee relationship that they can blossom into a person who has achieved their true potential. This is where Developmental Coaching can deliver something beyond the norm. As Psychologist Abraham Maslow said, 'What a man can be, he must be. This need we call self-actualisation.' Your job, as the coach, is to help in this perfectly natural process of actualising the innate potential we all possess. Developmental Coaching is a way for an individual, within cultural and systems contexts, to become all they can. As with the first session we are still really using the tools of conversation within a coaching frame to "get to know" the coachee. Emotionally they will benefit from feeling supported whilst you begin to create a map of where "they are at".

In practical terms you will be using the content of the first session throughout all of the rest. Goals will keep being set. This is a great reference point as to whether how they are getting on; but as you will see, it needs to be put into a broader context of development. I will say it again: use Goals in every session! Ok, now we are set to move on.

The lines

To begin, I want to give an overview of the theory for this session. When we talk of people's individual development, one fact becomes evident – we are all different. People can, therefore, develop differing abilities, and very often people become increasingly evolved within their *own particular field*. For instance, some people have natural abilities that automatically put a focus on one area of life, eg:

A politician may have brilliant communication and leadership qualities.

A sportsman may have great physical ability.

A businessman may be adept at making money.
An academic lecturer may have a highly developed mind.
A parent may have a high level of care and intuition.

It may be in many different fields of life that we come across particularly evolved people. The interesting observation is that you can have people who are highly developed in more than one of these areas – you don't have to focus only on one in order to develop. And if someone is looking at moving on in life, they will do best by looking at the different areas. For the coach, looking to help the coachee choose between the many roads they *could* take, it is necessary to know which roads they are already on (and yourself, as coach, will have already developed in many different ways and so will understand the principle), eg:
If a person has developed across a number of areas, they may have the ability:
to grasp something intellectually (cognitive)
talk about what they do (interpersonal skills)
have good body awareness whilst doing it, and
make a contribution to the social system that they live in

However, there is no personal development or coaching path that fits all, so rest assured that the coachees you come across will be about to choose their own direction. But if you want to know more about the coachee's profile (or focus of development within themselves), you can do so by looking at what is being done in their life and how these activities relate to different developmental lines (or ways that people can develop their abilities). So, this is really the essence of this session. Through knowing more about the coachee's life you are able to map out which lines they are developed in and developing.

As Howard Gardner (author of "Multiple Intelligences") says: "As human beings we have many different ways of *representing meaning, many kinds of intelligence.* Since the beginning of the last century, psychologists have spoken about a single intelligence that can be measured by an IQ test; my research has defined 8 or 9 human intelligences (linguistic; logical-mathematical, spatial, musical, bodily-kinesthetic, interpersonal, intrapersonal, naturalist, possibly an existential intelligence). We all possess these several intelligences, but no two of us - not even identical twins - possess the same profile of intelligences at the same moment."

Next let us look at the lines before returning to their application as a coach; I have chosen nine different developmental lines to show how different people may develop in particular areas:

cognitive – includes the ability to 'grasp' within the areas of mathematical thinking, logic, reasoning etc
affect (emotional) – this relates to feelings
interpersonal skills – this is the ability to relate to others (which, together with affect, are similar to 'emotional intelligence')
financial – relates to abilities to provide for needs
worldview – the appreciation of the differences between cultural perceptions
meditative awareness – concentration and awareness practices
natural talent and ability – this may include linguistic capability, musical talent etc
physiological development – sporting ability, physical awareness etc
moral development – includes level of concern for others

Let me use a metaphor which helps to explain the theory – imagine that a person is visually represented as a glass jar. In the jar are a collection of glass beads that represent the level of ability in a particular area. If the beads are stacked high, the level of ability is high – stacked low and it is low. Each level has a colour associated with it. From childhood, the colours progress to show the increase in development. But, and tying directly into the lines of development, not everyone develops in the same way. Some people will focus on different lines, lines which take them to a different level. So we have a jar that not only has beads of different colours, but also shows the focus of the person's development.

The contents of the jar represent, therefore, two main concepts. The first is the person's focus of development on the particular lines, eg moral, physiological, emotional etc. Secondly, it shows the person's level of development in any particular line (see the next chapter for more explanation). The best way to understand this is

to look at a few examples. In the examples, we use the following abbreviations:
C = Cognitive
A = Affect
I = Interpersonal
M = Moral development
T = Talent

Example 1
This situation represents someone who has developed a good level in four lines of development, eg cognitive, affect, interpersonal and a particular talent such as music (from which they earn their living):

```
C  A  I  M  T
C  A  I  M  T
C  A  I  M  T
C  A  I  M  T
```

Without one of these aspects, they may find themselves lacking the ability to be completely balanced. Or, looking at it another way, instead of balance we could see it show up as a challenge in life. There are almost certainly people that wouldn't be balanced in this way.

Example 2
This situation represents an academic who has the ability to know, but the inability to express their emotions (and feel challenged on a personal level when someone challenges what they believe in):

```
C
C        I
C  A  I
C  A  I  M
```

(Indicates a low level of affect (emotional capability).

It is even possible that someone who is great at communicating could be made up in a way that leads to a lack a sense of moral concern (M).

Emotional Quotient and lines of development

As a coach, you will have noticed over the past 20 years our culture has become less concerned with a person's Intelligence Quotient (IQ) as a gauge of their ability, becoming more concerned with their Emotional Quotient (EQ). At best, this will redress the balance because IQ was a prominent benchmark of abilities for a long time. In the same way though, focusing on any of these aspects alone may exclude other areas. Emotional intelligence consists of lines of development – primarily two lines, interpersonal and intrapersonal. In other words, it relates to how someone manages themselves and how they relate to those around them. But there is a danger in the EQ approach when it is taken out of context – that this is an aspect of individual development, not the whole focus of development. For example, if someone only focused on emotional development, they may gain a very high intuitive level of understanding, but fail to develop the higher level of cognitive ability that is needed by an evolving culture. They may, for instance, have a low level of technical skill that prevents them from attaining superb results at work. Similarly, they may become spiritually focused without a thorough grounding in interpersonal skills – this is often seen in the slightly woolly practitioner that cannot integrate into mainstream society.

Another very common condition in our culture is when people have a low affect or emotional level. When turning our attention to emotional intelligence, it is vital that we appreciate what low affect actually means in relation to emotions. For the coachee in particular, support in this area is one of the most useful things you may ever offer. We should never underestimate the role of a coach in helping people "get over" the feelings that are holding them back. This is not just changing the feeling but actually enabling the coachee to contextualise the feeling into a larger frame. This larger frame being a more comprehensive level of consciousness.

'Affect' then concerns your feelings and how you feel about how other people see you (so emotional stability would be included within this). It is a phenomenally important line of development as it also influences other lines. For example, people who are regularly challenged in a conversation may find that their "self-esteem" diminishes. In turn, they may fail to maintain their rational thinking – it is as if their sense of self is dependent on validation from the outside. When validation is no longer there, they experience a considerable challenge in keeping themselves together.

Example
This situation represents someone who would benefit from working on their interpersonal skills and their level of affect.

C
C   A
C   A   I   M
C   A   I   M   W

They may still be developing other lines of development (W).

The question then is how does this show up when you are coaching? It will be through examples. Emotional intelligence, and development of this, will come about when the person is able to relate at a higher level interpersonally with others, e.g. not just nodding a head to a neighbour, but developing a relationship with them; or not just focusing on communicating a task for an employee, but developing that individual; and changing their internal structure in relation to their emotions, e.g. having the ability to 'see through' emotions instead of 'being' these emotional states.

The same goes for the relationship with other people – if a person is in a relationship and finding it hard to communicate while feeling 'bad' about the situation, their lines of interpersonal and affect (emotions) could be developed. If you see someone experiencing difficulty in any area, it is a sign that they can benefit from developing a line of development.

Applications in coaching

With the understanding that personal development breaks down into many different developmental lines, as coaches *and* as people, we can notice which lines need more work once we know what to look out for. When working with the coachee, notice carefully which lines of development seem to be developed more and which seem to be developed less – or not at all. As you build up a map of the coachee, you will become more aware of which lines contain their greatest abilities.

In a practical sense, if someone is very abrupt with people, they may need to work on interpersonal skills. We all know this but may not think of it as a "line" as we may see it as a "behaviour", an "attitude" or possibly even a "skill". Someone else may have a low emotional ability and feel that people are manipulating them and so need to improve this area. Some others may have a limited cognitive capacity and find problem solving difficult, and so on.

This is an excellent starting place to understand how coaching can help develop the individual. Development of the coachee is largely about them taking a number of lines of development to higher levels, with your support. Whatever natural abilities or talents people have, they will have already started to move further along that ability/talent line. As long as there is progress, life can begin to feel less of a struggle as each stage of development solves a problem. And as coach, it is important to note that whatever the coachee previously struggled with was simply a reflection that a line of development needed further work, and that with further development, the coachee will increase their abilties in that area. In my experience, without developing a certain line, it is likely that little will change. As coach, you can point the coachee in the direction of the appropriate vehicle or learning experience that can help their development. Sometimes, however, this will not be comfortable for the individual. But your role, in this way more like a mentor, is not to help them feel more comfortable, it is to help them develop. This is where I see Developmental Coaching in this form becoming slightly different to many coaching approaches, especially when we want to "keep the client happy!" Instead, we need to have a strong enough relationship to allow a real stretch to occur.

Example: One coachee I was working with was feeling overloaded with work and her solution was to let go of the work at hand. This was not the essence of the problem and, in fact, this avoidance was actually detrimental as her manager considered that she was being lazy. I recall encouraging her to embrace the work load and learn to manage herself and her boss better so that the work came to her in a steady flow rather than so sporadically. This was not a comfortable process, especially as it was her that needed to develop a consistent approach with others, but the result was development instead of regression.

Interactions with others

I have begun to explain, from the viewpoint of the individual, how their lines of development make them who they are, but now let's turn our attention to development lines more in relation to interactions with other people. In this way, as coach, you will be able to help the coachee understand where other people are coming from and what they can do accordingly with what they find in front of them.

Lines of development in terms of finance and relationships, worldview or moral stance must take into account other people. A focus, for example, on understanding different perspectives of worldview will expand the reach of this line even further. Remember, people's abilities vary according to the level of development of their particular lines. So some interactions may seem challenging for a person who has a high level of interpersonal skills (but lower cognitive abilities), while another person who lacks interpersonal skills may be confused why someone can't understand something that requires high cognitive ability. All of this is determined by a level of development.

```
C       I
C   A   I   T
C   A   I   T
C   A   I   T
```

INTERACTION

```
C
C           T
C   A   I   T
C   A   I   T
C   A   I   T
```

To state it another way: when someone has a particular internal structure, that structure determines the type of interaction the person has. When the person's capacity in a developmental line increases, their interactions will change. In terms of the above example, one person may be unable to express their great understanding in a way that the other person can relate to, while the other may be more concerned about building the relationship rather than increasing the depth of cognitive understanding.

Through understanding this we can accept and be more tolerant in our moment-to-moment interactions with others. When we can intimately recognise where people 'are at', we can change our responses. The benefit being: these responses are often more suitable than those we would use if we did not appreciate what was going on.

At this point in the session with the coachee I am usually scribbling away these models in a notepad. Through engagement with the concept we are able to flesh out the content of their lives. They will often jump in straightaway with examples how this approach maps onto their own lives and relationships. This is great as it allows the coachee to really begin to internalise two aspects of Developmental Coaching. The first being the "lines"; the second being a gentle way into the "levels", as we will discuss more in later sessions.

Lines of development and the 4 Quadrants model

To recap, anything you do in your life requires a certain level of development in certain lines of development – this may be interpersonal, cognitive etc. There is, however, another aspect to introduce alongside the lines of development, i.e. 'balance'.

Certain activities in life focus on different areas more than others. Ken Wilber's 4 Quadrant model focuses around four main areas, i.e. mind, body (brain and behaviour), culture and social. It is suggested that all four of these areas must be considered, and within them a person can focus their time and effort. As I have stressed, my intention is to introduce the concept of "integral" in a very gentle fashion and not take it to its true depths in this book. With this freedom to use aspects of the approach, we can really focus on key developments.

When people focus their energies in any one area, the necessary developmental lines can be seen. For example, every time you have a conversation with someone else, you use your existing level of development in the interpersonal, affect, cognitive lines etc. So your ability within life's activities is determined by your development in whatever areas are crucial. Many personal development (or communication skills) courses are a blend of several skill sets that are relevant to many lines of development, e.g. improving relationships (e.g. rapport and appreciating individual differences), intrapersonal skills (self mastery), affect (e.g. 'having' emotions as opposed to being 'had' by them) and talents (learning to learn from others can help people to increase a line of development that is a 'talent', e.g. playing an instrument). Also, depending on the level of development of the person teaching it on the personal development course, it may even enable people to increase their moral development, e.g. through mentoring.

The following table shows a selection of activities in life's four main areas*. As coach, you may want to consider if the coachee is active in any similar activities. This, once again, will help you build a greater understanding of the coachee and where they are at.

Mind	**Body**
Intellectualising	Weight training
Meditation	Hatha Yoga, Dance
Exploration of feelings	Tai Chi
Cognitive	Things you do
Culture	**System within which money**
Community service	**is made**, eg Capitalist, Marxist,
Political service	solely agricultural
Team activities	And then operating within it

* Even though one activity has been emphasised in each area, all activities need four quadrants to exist.

So why is this important? It is said that if a person uses a balanced approach, they will develop their abilities far more than in any other way. Following a balanced approach, a person can use development lines to simultaneously develop their cognitive and affect (emotional) abilities, their interpersonal skills, their effect in the community and their place in the social system (e.g. influencing the business world). Here are a couple of quick examples:

Example 1
If someone excels as a philosopher (mind and brain activity), they need other people to discuss their views (culture) and a way for this to effect society at large (social system).

Example 2
As another example of how a balanced approach applies, it is like being able to practice yoga or a martial art, study and teach what you know, act within a community and earn a living from it. Or, run a business, put back into the community, learn more about themselves (internally) and behave in a way that expresses their values.

This approach takes account of the person's thoughts, feelings and body while extending them beyond themselves into society and culture.

People move upwards in a spiral towards reaching their own unique potential throughout these four areas – this is our own personal development path.

So, working with the coachee you can begin to introduce this concept. It helps in particular to tease apart the principle of the four domains - mind, body, culture and socitey. Many people simply don't have a map of individual/collective, interior/exterior in their head. When they are able with your support to start putting their lives into this model they are also seeing the greater benefits of an overarching model as well.

As coach, you have started to increase the map of appreciation that in turn can help the coachee follow their path through the domains. The challenges and decisions about which particular lines to follow are individual choices, with peoples' own unique personal history to colour them – the richness of experience that you have as coach will also bring its own unique exquisite flavour to how the coachee develops. This is very important for the way I have coached people. I am biased! I am opinionated! You too are not a passive observer in the process – your hand is on the coachee's shoulder as they stride forward. Sure, there are times you will simply allow what happens to happen, but you will also be the voice of reason when needed as well.

Finally I want to run through more specifics about how you can use the lines of development in a coaching context. As you read, begin to consider the people around you and maybe what lines of development they are using most and to what degree. This will aid translation of the principles across into your own life and your interactions with others.

Clearly, the line of development that is called 'physiology' can seriously affect health. But to be consistent, and at the risk of being boring, health will exist in all four quadrants, e.g. how someone manages their feelings (affect) will impact their quality of health.
One coachee I was working with found they were anxious after mealtimes but unsure why. On exploration, we raised awareness by asking questions about their eating habits over the past few years. Their physiological awareness began to become increased and their

response to certain foods and drinks was monitored more closely. The resultant information about the cause seems so obvious now! They found that drinking coffee at the end of the meal increased their heart rate and this was the feelings associated with the emotion of anxiety. It was that simple.

On another occasion, one coachee found that, due to their coaching sessions, they could increase their levels of personal flexibility to gaining fulfilment. In other words, the "bad habits" had to go! The coachee was finding that they could no longer find any meaning in what they were doing, despite being 'good' with people and achieving excellent results as a self-employed man. They began to look at developing additional lines of development (including moral) with support. It was then that he began to realise that personal fulfilment was not enough – he needed to turn his attention outward. Through the interaction, the coachee was enabled to explore how serving the community would not only rejuvenate himself, but aid in the development of others. As a result, the coachee began to contribute to the community that had supported his business for many years. This was done through utilisation of online mechanisms, including charity sites and applications on facebook. Interestingly, this idea of greater satisfaction, or even any satisfaction, coming from a focus on helping others has come up many times in coaching sessions. So often though, people really need to take a step back to work out a) the issue, b) acknowledge it and then c) the options they can consider. The coach's role is to see which lines the coachee is neglecting and may ask if they believe that they could enjoy exploring options that could lead to their development. Sometimes the coachee will be reluctant to move, but with suitable 'holding', in time they will.

As I mentioned earlier, interpersonal and intrapersonal skills are key elements in a relationship. The quality of a relationship is determined by many factors including, how we manage ourselves and the way we communicate verbally and non-verbally with others. Take the example of a string of mis-communications whereby the message you intended to give was not the one that was received. Sound familiar? For instance, you may have wanted to create a good impression of yourself by being confident in either a family or business situation but instead you were told later that you came across as aloof and arrogant. In this case, the coach may ask the coachee to look at what they did and the response they received. They may then discuss how the coachee can approach the situation differently. For instance, the coach may look at how the coachee can adapt their personal style to approach a partner, their family, a colleague or a client in a more suitable fashion. Through concerted effort the coachee may make changes to their language, voice tone and physical presence. In one case, the coachee developed the ability to automatically adapt themselves to the environment's needs, for example, altering their voice tone to suit clients' voices on the end of the telephone. Instead of a rigid 'this is me' response, the coachee learned to approach people in a more appropriate way. This will take self-awareness on the part of the coachee as well as the desire to change – even though the example is very simple, it essentially requires the development of interpersonal and intrapersonal abilities.

Let's us finally consider the idea of "talent". Whether the talent is sport, art or writing (to name but a few), the role of the coach is to aid the talent's fruition. It is likely that the coach has an enlightened self-interest in seeing this talent displayed well – and this self-interest takes the form of a warm glow of satisfaction that the coach has helped someone achieve their true potential. As a Developmental Coach, it is your role to see when talent is being wasted – it could be within the context of a business role as much as any other. If someone has the ability to listen and appreciate their colleagues' needs but remain at a low management level, even this could be seen as a wasted talent. But it could be anything from music to teaching to sport.

In the world of sport, with one coachee, I recall looking at ensuring the coachee was able to support themselves financially during the initial period of their talent's development. This was a growth of the coachee's 'business' line. Eventually this line of development developed further so that the coachee was able to take their talent further into the business world. Not only were they competing to a high level of athletics, but also going into organisations and giving premium rate speeches on their personal experiences A good result for all!

That wraps up this session. Next session we will look at the levels of development we touched on earlier. This is where the "development" bit really kicks in.

Questions for reflection
What are the coachee's obvious strengths?
Do you have a map of the developmental lines that are operating? If certain ones were developed, would it help to solve the challenges they presented?
What do you see that the coachee does not?
What are they shying away from?

Session 3

Levels of consciousness

Levels of consciousness

In this chapter we look at the main transformations that can be aided by a Developmental Coaching approach. I approach it knowing my potential pool of coachees will generally be within these levels, but I know myself that people can be both above and below. I have chosen not to give a full explanation on the theory of levels of consciousness as the recommended reading will do far more to aid understanding. So won't be attempting to explain the "highest reaches of consciousness", I'll leave that one to Ken Wilber et al. Instead, I will look to make this as practical and user friendly as possible for the most likely of circumstances. This is still going to take us up to dialectical thinking so, don't fret 99.9% of people will find this useful.

I have to admit, when I began teaching these levels in larger groups, I recall some blank faces! "Levels" can be a little tricky but this approach will operate as a kind of framework to consciousness that is a handy talking point with the coachee, as well as one for you to use yourself. It should be very easy to grasp, especially when you combine it with the later chapters. I know how much people into coaching enjoy "skills based" approaches; this way I think we bridge theory with a practical approach.

Jean Baker Miller in Toward a New Psychology of Women explains that "Psychological problems are not so much caused by the unconscious as by deprivations to full consciousness. If we had paths to more valid consciousness all along through life, if we had more accurate terms in which we conceptualise what was happening, if we had more access to the emotions produced, and if we had ways of knowing our true options – we could make better programmes for action. Lacking full consciousness, we create out of what is available." With that purpose in mind, the following explains the three main transitions a Developmental Coach can help a coachee achieve to expand their consciousness and choices. As a coach, you may never need to label them as they are below, but if you do you can 'point' at yourself at the same time you can begin to see when these levels are being accessed within yourself. If you decide to discuss with them this coaching approach explicitly (as I often will do), it is the ability to have the appropriate language that will also give you and your coachees a common understanding of what is going on. In the meantime the language will enable you to empathise more with where the person 'is at' as well as where they could be.

Robert Kegan, a compassionate writer and academic, sees that at each stage of our development we construct meaning in the world differently – we make meaning differently at each stage. He begins, "If you want to understand another person in some fundamental way you must know where the person is in his or her evolution" and he continues that the first goal in this understanding is "how the other person composes his or her private reality." This, as you can see, is very much aligned with the process we are taking in this book. And it is the levels to this reality, or making of meaning, not just the thoughts and feelings that could be at a given level, that we next turn our attention.

I have based this section on Robert Kegan's work but have also used psychologist Piaget's traditional terms to describe the stages. Once again, I start with an overview of the theory, but interlace coaching as a theme throughout. The examples of 'leaps', developments or transformations are my own.

'As if' to 'what if?
To begin, the first transformation a coach may be involved in is the transformation from 'as if' to 'what if' thinking. Briefly, the difference between concrete operational thinking (or, 'as if' thinking) and formal operation thinking (or, 'what if' thinking) can be illustrated by a test. You will remember this from school: You have three test tubes of clear liquids labelled A, B and C. You ask two people (one at the 'as if' stage and one at the 'what if' stage) to find out which two liquids, when mixed together, become cloudy. The 'as if' person will plough into the problem without much pre-thought or consideration, and try different combinations until they find the two test tubes that make the cloudy liquid. We can probably relate to this when we "can't be bothered" which is exactly what happens i.e. we use this very limited type of thinking. Conversely, the 'what if?' person will take a different approach – they will think 'what if?' I mix A and B, A and C, C and A and C and B. In other words, they will prepare a hypothesis and test the hypothesis out – 'what if?'.

Robert Kegan beautifully encapsulates 'as if' as, "The concrete operational [person] explores the limits of the world, but within the terms of the evolutionary truce. From a more evolved point of view we might say it is an exploration along a plane without recognition of the third dimension." Remember the flatland story in the Introduction? This is the same reference. When transformation occurs, the former concrete operational individual will no longer act 'as if' in a realm of what is, they begin to consider what might be, i.e. 'what if?' Increasingly using 'what if?' thinking opens up the individual's capacity to generate more options within a closed system by using a theory.

Let's now look at a couple of examples. In a game of pool, the 'what if?' thinker will usually work out the optimum entry and exit angles for the balls bouncing off the cushion, using their mathematical understandings of reflection. On the other hand, the 'as if' thinker will usually just 'give it a go,' without utilizing a theory. Similarly in a coaching context we are not just looking at the results but also starting to build a map of the causes. This is a movement to 'what if?' thinking starts during our teenage years but is often not held as a stable level of consciousness. Because the 'as if' stage is very much 'self' and 'needs' orientated, the 'as if?' individual will do little or nothing to take account other peoples' viewpoints. This can, as you would guess, cause problems. Conversely, the stable 'what if?' individual can hold other people's viewpoints while not losing the knowledge and appreciation of their own needs, e.g. the 'what if?' thinks 'what if? I behave or act in a certain way – how will others feel and how will I feel? This is a prerequisite to entering into high-quality interpersonal relationships.

So, the shift to 'what if?' thinking is more encompassing and extends beyond the preceding stage. It is only if and when the development to this stage is negotiated and stabilised that stages of later development can be supported. This then is the first shift/transformation that the coach can support the coachee through. If the coachee is operating without much thought to the consequences of their actions for self and others, the coach may ask, 'What do you think will happen if you do this?' By repeating, this and similar questions, the coachee will begin to draw a bigger map of the territory they are operating within. I know it sounds very simple but it also allows for a degree of reasoning that may enable the coachee to make a profound difference in their lives. Beforehand, the map, put simply, may not have been drawn.

It is crucial that the coachee completes this first transition because, unless there is a stable base to build on, the construction of self will be less stable as we move onwards. As coach, there is no need to point your finger at the coachee's level of development, but the movement from concrete operational thinking to formal operational thinking is frequently not completed in all contexts by the coachee. While this stage is not the most fundamental and initial of stages (which I shall look at relating to the session on Adaptations), it is a commonly needed leap for the individual to feel more at ease within the culture. They could feel they are truly drowning if not. Really, as we will see, this shift is absolutely necessary (but not sufficient) within Western culture to live a satisfactory life. If the coachee has not yet made this transition, the coach should 'hold' them and explore with them the options at their level of being. As Wilber says, "every time you imagine different outcomes, every time you see a possible future different from today's, every time you dream a dream of what might be, you are using formal operational awareness."

'What if?' to 'Full what if?' or "Self-authoring"
The next transformation, on which Developmental Coaching focuses, is what Robert Kegan calls 'self-authoring' (Piaget called this full formal operational thinking), or 'full what if?' thinking. We can express this initial development as one of objectifying the internal world of thoughts, feelings or emotions. No longer is the individual 'had' by their emotions – they begin to 'have' them. This is the key phrase for this transformation and one that you will use with a coachee time and time again. It sums up the concept incredibly well. The resultant transformation can be highly motivating as it can free the person from much emotional instability.

At the 'what if?' stage it is difficult to know one's own mind and to follow one's own dreams independent from what is expected of you within your role. Carol Gilligan wrote that there seems to be "the yearning to be included, to be part of, close to, joined with, to be held, admitted, accompanied" and also "the yearning to be independent and autonomous, to experience one's own distinctness, the self-choseness of one's direction, one's individual integrity." If 'what if?' thinking is an absolute prerequisite for modern living, 'full what if?' thinking is emerging as a seriously desirable level of consciousness. At this "self authoring" stage the individual's internal world is seen as an object, or in other words, the person is no longer embedded within their thoughts and feelings, but knows them to be separate – the dependence on binding relationships and the peer group of the 'what if?' stage has been transcended (but remains important). This is a stage of 'psychological independence' or autonomy, but that does not mean that the person needs to be isolated. As Kegan says, "deciding for myself" does not mean "deciding by myself." At this stage, there is a change from taking on a role (within a job or as a parent) and then taking it to its natural end – instead the individual takes on an authorship role in what end is reached. This is the emergence of an independent thinker who can reflect upon their roles within society and see themselves as someone other than the sum of their roles. The individual has developed through and beyond the role-taking level of consciousness and now as their new self they will take on a new perspective as the organiser of the roles – a coordinator that no longer sees conflicts as outside themselves, but has brought them inside. This is the realm of self reflexive consciousness – being able to see the workings of one's own mind and know that this is the realm that much conflict can be resolved. This is a stage, once obtained, any individual will appreciate. Through the process, many of my own clients, as coachees, have felt freer and more "together" than ever before.

The Developmental Coach will help stabilise the movement to this stage by aiding the individual to decide what they want to achieve for themselves – how they want to live their dreams while still recognizing the importance of their relationships. At this stage relationships become very important as a way of defining the self. As the coach, you will also encourage the coachee to reflect on their thoughts and feelings about certain issues and leave them to come to their own conclusions – or at least make them think about their conclusions before discussing then further. You will avoid telling them what to expect and the coachee may be surprised with what they find!

'Full what if? to 'What, what if?' or Post-formal operational thinking or Dialectical thinking

Beyond the 'full what if? (self-authoring) stage of thinking, but only when the coachee is ready, the Developmental Coach can assist their development even further. Obviously it will depend on where the coachee "is at", so this could relate to either the same individual over a long period of time or to totally different coachees.

Post-formal operational thinking, or 'what what if?' thinking will then emerge, revealing a cognitive capacity for cross contextualisation. So, this is the key element we need to discuss in relation to this stage of consciousness. It can be a little tricky but I'll see what I can do...
Cross contextualisation is when the individual no longer takes on different roles in life, but takes 'the theme of their life', their centredness, into different contexts. This is the awakening of dialectical thinking (or as Ken Wilber calls it 'vision logic'). This is a perfectly natural emergence that is open to us all, and as Wilber says, we don't even have to master the earlier stages - just stabilize them.

Let me explain a little more about this stage to make it more solid. Formal operational thinking i.e. 'what if?' thinking, is a problem solving stage, but one of the ways formal operational thinking can and will fail is when the individual has to deal with a high degree of contradiction. For instance (and using an example from Kaisa Puhakka), if a physicist is looking at physical reality, they will find evidence that physical reality is a 'wave' and, at the same time a 'particle'. This contradiction cannot be resolved at the 'what if?' (or 'full what if?' – which is largely the same, just more mature). Instead, the physicist somehow goes beyond the basis, and instead looks to the theory that yields the results of either a 'wave' or a 'particle'. This way these contradictions are 'held in mind', that is, this process is seen as a way of unifying opposites – this is dialectical thinking.
If you would like to know more on the contradiction then search Youtube for "Dr Quantum's Double Slit Experiment"! It is a fun one.

In formal operational thinking (what if?) the identity of the object must be fixed in order to be worked with at that time (the system is closed – the variables are known- as in the mixing of the testubes).

At the 'What, what if?' stage, however, the variables are not seen as being fixed – they are seen within a space that allows them to be as they are. This stage 'possesses not just a new cognitive capacity (what, what if?) – it also involves a new sense of identity..., with new desires, new drives, new perceptions.' And as Wilber points out, this is the stage of integration. It would be reasonable to expect that this is the stage that the Developmental Coach can aim his coachees towards (and this is self actualization in Maslow's terms) but it may be up to the coachee to put the hours of study in to really "grasp it". Dialectical thinking is, as I say, tricky to explain but I hope to have given you some initial ideas about how "it looks".

Having kept the explanations of these transitions brief, the examples below will further help you to 'place' them in your coaching life and in life in general. I have chosen to show one developmental stage per example but all the stages are present within each area – in fact all stages are present within all areas of life (mind, body, culture and behaviour) and within all the lines of development that exist within all these areas. But let's keep it straightforward and practical as in this section I intend only point the way for you to find your own points of application, otherwise I am both restricting and telling you something 'as if'.

In the region of health, and in this example it will be largely emotional and mental health, I want to offer an explanation of the development from 'as if' (concrete operational thinking) to 'what if?' (formal operational thinking). On one occassion, a coachee was having a challenge with a partner who was not yielding to their emotional needs, or maybe even desires. This was causing them emotional turmoil and even led to a physiological manifestation of health problems such as bowel complaints and lack of sleep. They had tried to express their needs time and time again, but it was always with the same result. They simply were not heard. Effectively, all the translations had failed. As is indicative of 'as if' thinking, the coachee was operating from a place that was orientated around their self needs – they were failing to appreciate the point of view of their partner. The harder they tried, the more they failed and the more entrenched they had become in their own view- they were, in their words, "banging their head against a brick wall." During the coaching session, and related to the other family member, I was able to gently talk the coachee into 'walking a mile in the other family member's shoes'. Initially the coachee was reluctant to see the other person's viewpoint, but with questions such as 'When you are talking, what do you think is happening for them?' and 'If you were listening to this in their position, what would you be thinking and feeling?', the coachee was able to achieve a movement to 'what if?' thinking. In this case, instead of acting 'as if' only the coachee's needs are important, 'what if?' the coachee started thinking about what is happening for those around them.

It is incredibly simple but this method effectively resulted in the coachee seeing something they hadn't previously seen, which in turn reduced the internal tension. The coach's role is to support this psychological development and in this case, and over time in this case, the coachee also managed to improve the relationship through increased understanding and appreciation.

Next I will give an example of movement from 'what if?' to 'full what if?' thinking i.e. self-authoring (a phrase I love). Robert Kegan is a great source of examples of differences between the ways of thinking at the different levels. For instance, he comments in "In over our heads" that many management books point to differences in employee approach. So, using this as an example, let's look at two different approaches within a business context. One employee may, for instance, ask for specific details about goals, criteria for achievement, reward and evaluation. In contrast, another employee may both be mindful of their employer's view, but "has his/her own contribution to make toward understanding the goals, planning for their accomplishment, and evaluating their outcome." As Kegan points out, the second employee is operating with 'full what if?' thinking. This is not something that is a learned skill – it has come from the emergence of a way of being. This is when the employee is acting in a way that is synonymous to being self-employed. This is a handy principle in coaching sessions! Would a person be as they are if they were self-employed?! In the business context, when we 'employ the self-employed', the role of manager becomes quite different as there is a high degree of autonomy within the staff.

In a coaching context, the coach can aid the coachee to develop this self-employed way of thinking by helping them take more responsibility for the form of their employment. They are no longer pinned to a role that is given, but they instead develop within that role (and in turn that role will actually develop). This helps a shift from 'what if' to 'full what if?' Also, the individual will act in a more 'steady' manner, with less hijacking of rogue emotional states as a secondary consequence of the state of consciousness. This is a key area as there becomes a self that internally manages all of the other selves. The sub-personalities (as you will see) we all have come under the charge and management of a greater more encompassing 'self'. The individual is able to see these sub-personalities instead of the individual moving from state to state without a cohesive sense of self that is over and beyond all those states.

Frequently in a coaching sense the coach will help the coachee 'reflect on' instead of 'acting out' when an emotional impulse presents itself. This will lead to the individual 'steadying up'. It also leads to a great internal freedom from the sub-personalities (that often appear as inner voices or emotions) that can otherwise take over the show for a time before returning from whence they came. For those of you who are familiar with meditation techniques used to observe the objects of mind, then this is an excellent point to introduce them to a coachee. It is at the cusp of this stage they most appreciate how they can objectify the contents of mind instead of being "subject" to them i.e. embedded within them.

Looking next at a shift from 'full what if?' to 'what what if?' thinking, Michael Basseches superb book Dialectical Thinking gives an example in the context of relationships. This gives us another angle where you can look at application areas. The 'what if?' (formal operational) approach to relationships tends to see that people are quite fixed and have rigid traits, whereas the 'what what if?' (dialectical) way of thinking is quite different. As Basseches says, this approach could "begin with the assumption that my traits are not fixed and that the relationships I enter will shape who I am and who my partner is." He continues that when this is the case in the relationship, both individuals will be "evaluating whether the relationship is evolving in ways which allow both of us to develop as individuals while it continues to develop as a relationship." So, what does this mean for coaching? When assisting this transformation as a coach in the relationship context, it is your role to support the emergence of thinking that people are "created by the relationship" as much as they "create the relationship". This can lead to higher levels of fulfilment for the coachee as they are no longer ego bound in such a rigid fashion. If they considered themselves to 'a serious person' they might have shied away from someone who was 'playful' as a partner, as they would have seen this as a conflict to their style. But at this 'what what if?' (dialectical) stage, the coachee may be able to explore their own 'playfulness' as is brought out by the interactions with the other. This, as Basseches points out, can quite dramatically change the perspective of the person we used to be (in this case, 'I am a serious person'). Taking it further, during relational challenges, instead of the usual blame, guilt and regret type responses, the individual at this level may ask, 'How does the relationship need to change in response to the changes it has brought about in us in order for it to continue?' So, as we draw this section on "levels" to a close, let's consider this principle as the view is rather different to the earlier stages. For a coachee, they will not only look at changes they make in themselves, they will also look at the changes they make to the *relationship itself* because of the ongoing developments *within themselves. This is a dynamic interplay of the two selves within a dynamic relationship.* You see? This is when Developmental Coaching begins to suggest something that is not just about changing behaviours. This is about consciousness.

Questions for reflection
Do you map people's levels of consciousness? What evidence do you collect? How will you collect more evidence and build a better map?
Think about those around you. What transformations have they made in the last five years?
As a coach, what can you do to help the movement between levels?

Session 4

Adaptations to life

Adaptations to life

In our last session we began to put some flesh on the bones of consciousness, expressed through several developmental shifts. This session is one of my favourites as it makes expressions of the levels of consciousness tangible in a way you may not have thought about. In Sigmund Freud's view, mental health is the capacity to work and to love; it is this type of fundamental engagement in life – working and loving – that can determine whether a person is living a rich and fulfilling life, or one steeped in anguish. For the Developmental Coach, the question that requires careful consideration is this: 'What are the indications of a healthy adaptation to life?' or putting it another way, how do you know *how a person views the world from their actions?*

This is rather a long session (in the book anyway) as it covers all of the adaptations available. Bear with it - it is worth it! The good news for a coach is how practical this approach will be in everyday life as well as in every coaching session - you will get a lot out of this personally. As a coach, the stages of adaptation will begin to occupy your attention as you engage in and reflect on your interactions with coachees. Note then, the adaptations listed below are available to us all and a good look inside ourselves and into our own ways of dealing with life is a prerequisite to work with others in this area. Without considerable self-exploration you may not see them at all, or maybe you will be seeing outside what is actually within yourself.

In the last chapter we looked at the four main levels of consciousness – 'as if?', 'what if?', 'full what if? and 'what what if?', i.e. concrete operational, formal operational, full formal operational and post formal operational thinking/dialectical. You will choose what name you want to use with coachees or clients; I will continue to use most of them, so you can become more easily familiar as the framework develops "in your head" so to speak.
As the self journeys through these levels of consciousness, it needs to find a way of dealing with the life it creates and experiences. Like anything that perceives itself as separate, it needs defences to hold and maintain itself. These 'defences' or 'adaptations' (these words are interchangeable in this context) are the methods we use

to maintain a sense of balance at a certain level – they are kind of distortions or possibly even 'lies' we tell ourselves that serve this end. R D Laing saw these as 'knots' (which is a little friendlier) and used the following to describe the lies we most often don't know we tell ourselves:

The range of what we think and do
is limited by what we fail to notice.
And because we fail to notice
that we fail to notice
there is little we can do
to change
until we notice
how failing to notice
shapes our thoughts and deeds.

There is a spectrum to these adaptations that spans from the most primitive through to the most mature. All other things being equal, as we grow and develop there is a natural emergence of the more mature mechanisms. These mature mechanisms are more 'acceptable' as ways of being in the world and for the possessor they are more expansive and somehow more inclusive. If we must lie, the more mature lies are better; and as such, the quality of a person's life can be judged by the adaptations they use. Let us try not to knot in ways that stop us enjoying life!

For coaching, I suggest it is in large part the person's adaptations that determine whether they will be a success or not. Being a success (defining this as 'achieving your dreams') will be determined by the person's internal structure and there is nothing more important as an indication of this than the defences they apply. So clearly this is a great "set of tools" for working with the coachee. You will be able to adapt and apply this as you get more used to the concepts. Before expanding on some of the coaching applications, however, I will first give an overview of the stages of adaptations.

Stages of adaptation

George Vaillant, author of *Adaptation to Life*, was involved in research that studied 'healthy' individuals over a thirty year period. This study, called the *Grant Study*, tracked 268 healthy men from college students into adulthood. Ok, it was only men, not women, but it still makes a great read.

The result is a beautiful movie-like journey through many of these men's lives – through their problems and anguish, and their considerable joys. On reading *Adaptation to Life*, the reader is awakened to a new depth of richness in those around them. And even though it is never wise, nor kind, to point at someone's adaptations directly, the ability to notice how a person adapts to life becomes a great aid in supporting the growth of that individual. Each stage of Vaillant's suggested adaptations relates to one of the levels of consciousness we discussed earlier (with the addition of a 'pre-as if' stage).

Level of consciousness	Piaget's term	Stage of adaptation
Pre-as if	Pre-operational	'Psychotic'
As if	Concrete operational	'Immature'
What if?		
Full What if?	Formal operational	'Neurotic'
Self-authoring		
What what if?	Post-Formal operational	'Mature'
Dialetical thinking		

As the table uses words that may cause concern or offence, especially 'psychotic', 'immature' and 'neurotic', I will explain their meaning in this context. As a person develops from a child they move up the spiral of development, taking on the associated defences for a specific level of consciousness. So for a child aged two, the psychotic adaptations are a suitable level adaptation (they can have some crazy fantasies!). For a child age six, the immature adaptations are a suitable level (they can huff and puff and try to punish you, in their way). As an adult – and these are the most common in adults – the neurotic adaptations are suitable (with everyone having their funny quirks), and for the later stages in life, there are the mature defences (seeking the expression of *who they are*).

Now expanding this out a little, below is an overview of the stages and types of adaptations within in each stage.

Adaptations

	Adaptations	
	Denial and delusion	
Stage I – Psychotic	Narcissism	
	Borderline condition	
	Projection	
Stage II Immature	– Hypochondriasis	
	Passive aggressive and acting out	
	Intellectualisation	
Stage III Neurotic	– Repression and dissociation	
	Displacement and neurotic denial	
	Reaction formation	
	Suppression	
Stage IV – Mature	Anticipation	
	Altruism and humour	
	Sublimation	

As we are considering a developmental approach, we must discuss the earliest stages to some degree, but I will focus more attention on stages II, III and IV because, as a coach, you can do more about these adaptations. I have based some of this on the *Grant study* findings, but have chosen a selection of adaptations and sometimes blended two similar adaptations together. Also, based on the work of Engler, Brown and Wilber (from *Transformations of Consciousness*) I have adapted the earliest stage of adaptation to include two classic defences that Vaillant did not code with the same language. These are 'narcissism' and 'borderline condition'- both of which I have come across in coaching sessions.

Stage I adaptations
Stage I adaptations are perfectly healthy as a young child, but not for a normally developed adult, where it is the most distorted view:
Denial and delusion
Individuals who apply these adaptations alter the reality in which they live. But, as Vaillant says, they will appear 'crazy' to any adult observing them in another adult. 'Denial' denies the external world. 'Delusion' often involves persecution (and is frequently paranoid in nature).

Narcissism
Similar to distortion (using Vaillant's term), the individual grossly reshapes the external world for their own needs. This defence keeps the individual at the centre of their universe. This is the defence of the 'all important'.

Borderline condition
This adaptation occurs when a person is cannot hold an object as both 'good' and 'bad' at the same time. Internally the individual 'splits' them into two halves, 'good' and 'bad', and cannot see the same object as both good and bad, e.g. the mother was such an object when we were children.

In an adult, these adaptations are crippling – it is even possible that such an individual will have a record of mental health problems if they sustain these adaptations over a long period. But as a coach it is more interesting to look at small traits within oneself or within the behaviours of others that point to elements of the self being stuck at this level. The person, then, is not always stabley at a certain level of development and employing the level of adaptation that corresponds to that level. Instead, there can be trace elements that remain at a lower level. So, keep your eyes open!

As an example, delusional paranoia could come from narcotic induced experiences that leave the person twisting their reality to make sense of the experiences they had. For instance, if the individual experiences a sense of persecution, they may create a reality of some kind of 'plot' against them, that their telephone is tapped, sinister forces in the universe are trying to corrupt their thinking or there are fairies at the bottom of the garden that give them messages. For the Developmental Coach, serious denial and delusion adaptations are best left for medical experts. However, if the coachee's denial and delusion traits are mild– and a heavy dose of superstition can often fall into a delusional magical category that is not far away from these – then as the coach you may want to support them through reading. Through this process the coachee's self may let go of that level of adaptation and bring themselves together to a higher level.

Narcissism, on the other hand, is far more common in our culture than we may choose to believe. This is the defence of 'me'. This is not even 'me' and my family – it is just about 'me'. As Wilber puts it, it is "the overestimation of self as measured against the devaluing of others, that marks the narcissistic defence." So, this defence is not about high self-esteem, it is an imbalance in the view between the importance of the self and others'. Narcissism is not about striving for individual achievement and success – this would only be narcissistic if the individual ignores the importance of other people (and maybe even their goals and dreams) along the way. As coach, this is actually your key to helping someone reduce the amount of narcissism present within themselves. If they don't, it is likely that people around them will feel undervalued and unappreciated, and this will seriously affect the individual's life. The main way for someone to grow through a high degree of narcissism is to develop increasing levels of concern for others. The first place to begin is in proximity – family and workplace.

A borderline condition is a way of preventing something 'good' being engulfed by its 'bad' attributes. It is an adaptation that keeps the parts, good and bad, separate and means that the individual is unable to see that someone or something is both good and bad simultaneously. They 'split' the object into two and then internally oscillate between two contradictory opinions. One minute 'they are, or it is, the best thing in the world' and the next minute 'they are, or it is, the worst thing in the world.' Really, this should be dealt with by a therapist if it is a major trait (the therapist will help build the ego to a point where the individual can integrate the two opposing halves). As a coach, it is worthwhile remembering that this adaptation exists because it may explain why someone's opinion oscillates between two opposing views. If the person is otherwise healthy, you may choose to ask them to consider how what they are looking at has both good and bad aspects – so bringing together what was previously kept apart.

In this overview of Stage I defences, I have suggested minimal intervention by the coach. However, these defences are more common than we may think, so I do consider it relevant that the coach has an understanding of their existence. As we shall see more and more, it is the individual's adaptations/defences that determine if they live their dreams – if they are stopping themselves in some way, their defences will have a major role. Even when the individual has the 'intention' to achieve a goal, their adaptive needs (i.e. the need of the having the defence mechanisms) may override that goal being achieved – the first stage of freeing ourselves is when we can see these lies or distortions in ourselves.

To recap, adaptations will change as the individual develops, and a natural progression from Stage I to Stage II will occur at an early age. This is where we go next.

Stage II adaptations

Adaptations theory suggests that, throughout a healthy life, there is a continuum of adaptations to life and a flow of the self through the stages of adaptation as the individual grows and develops. It is when the individual gets stuck at a lower stage of development and bears out its associated adaptations, that we may find ourselves as coach to an 'emerging adult self'. The adult can develop through their less mature adaptations to become a more fulfilled, less conflicted, kinder and more caring individual. The former child becomes able to be more appreciative of the needs of those around them and develops a healthier view of life. At each stage of development, and with the use of every adaptation, the world appears to 'be' a certain way. This internal subjective experience gives meaning to life. For that unwell adult who has regressed to stage I defences such as delusion, they may see the world in a paranoiac way – their view of the world is determined by this level of consciousness and their corresponding defence. If the individual can move on from this adaptation, they will adapt the way they see the world as the self lets go of their former way of being.

It is likely that the adult adaptations we see at stage II, i.e. 'immature' defences, will be healthier than those of stage I. So even though we call these 'immature', they are still a step on from the most primitive defences that went before them. Stage II adaptations are called 'immature' but they are really healthy adaptations for anyone aged up to 15 years, and from a coaching perspective, immature adaptations tend to extend into adulthood as well.

As a coach, appreciation of this stage of development – at the 'as if' or concrete-operational (con-op) level of consciousness – will help provide a basis to a suitable approach with the coachee. But they may not be the easiest to manage because, for the coachee, the way they view the world is through this adaptive form and they cannot just be 'given up'; otherwise the coachee will be unable to make sense of the world. As a Developmental Coach, it is your role to help and support the emergence of the next stages of adaptive development in the same way as we were talking about emerging levels in the last session. So, do you see the pieces starting to come together in how you will operationalise the theory? In the same way as we looked at the emergence of different levels of consciousness – 'as if' to 'what if? to 'full what if? to 'what what if?' – adaptations arise at the same time since they are emergent at these levels. If someone is predominantly 'as if' (con-op) as their current way of being, then the stages of adaptation available to them will only be stage I and stage II. Even though there is potential for later stages to emerge, they do not have the cognitive capacity for them to be realised as yet. The coachee will be using these adaptations, or defences, as a way of making meaning in the world around them. This is great from a coaching perspective as you can use their "display" to "know where they are at". In order for them to move on, they must evolve through each stage, letting go of the previous way of being as they go. That is what you can help them to do through your sessions.

The coach, as I will discuss toward the end of the chapters on adaptations, will find that the coachee's adaptive mechanisms are truly a clear indication of the life they live. This is why this section will prove so useful to you. The healthier and more developed the adaptations, the greater the opportunity for living a 'good' life. As a Developmental Coach, it can be your aim to support and aid the coachee's development so they too can have a 'good' life. In return, the coachee will also find that their life quality extends out to others more and more. Stage II is, however, not a healthy adaptation for an adult, and the rest of this chapter discusses the three main manifestations of defence at this level.

Projection, hypochondriasis and passive aggressive behaviour adaptations relate more to interrelationships with others than to how an individual relates to themselves. As these adaptations manifest themselves at the 'as if' (con op) level of consciousness, the individual will have great difficulty fully appreciating other people's position because of their limited ability to 'put themselves in another's shoes' (which is a key aspect of this level of consciousness). As a result, it is not surprising that this level of consciousness could lead to difficulties for an adult who has the corresponding adaptations. The main adaptations will involve interpersonal exchanges and this is a clue for how to move on from these adaptations. The stage II adaptations are briefly explained below.

Projection
Vaillant describes this as "attributing one's own unacknowledged feelings to others." Much of the world's prejudice and 'witch hunting' comes from this defence. When it is 'not me, it's them' the individual may start building a case against individuals or groups that support their own negative feelings.

Hypochondriasis
This adaptation manifests itself in the movement of emotional needs into a physical illness. If a person is lonely, instead of making demands on people around them more openly, they aim to gain attention through illness. This way they gain the attention they so much desire.

Passive aggressive behaviour (and acting out)
This is when an individual acts "aggressively towards others expressed indirectly and ineffectively through passivity or directed against the self". Vaillant mentions in his summary of adaptations that it can include failures, procrastinations or illnesses that affect others as well as the individual. It may also manifest as silly and provocative behaviour.
The individual might also turn this aggression outward and it could be seen as active aggressive behaviour and delinquency (including self infliction, drug abuse and temper tantrums).

Stage II adaptations can often be seen as the least savoury of the adaptations as the main impact is in the realm of relationships with others. Whereas Stage I adaptations are seen as crazy, stage II adaptations are seen as damned rude and offensive. As a teenager a degree of flexibility may be given (and certainly a peer group will have these adaptations), but they are difficult to accept from an adult.

In coaching, the main way of supporting someone's growth and development from stage II adaptations into more healthy ones is quite simple. As the main problem lies in the lack of appreciation of relationships, let's say in passive aggressive behaviour, this is also the realm of the solution. It is actually through developing relationships and appreciating (not being told) how one's own actions impacts on others, that this level of consciousness can be released, allowing the next stage to emerge. The movement from 'as if' to 'what if?' thinking (con-op to form-op) will occur as the person starts to consider alternative viewpoints more and more. The ability to put oneself in another person's shoes will help the individual appreciate the impact of their actions. Then, when a decision to take action arises that could have a negative impact on another, the person will think through 'what if?' they behave in a certain way.

I said that Stage II adaptations are not healthy in normal adult conditions, but they are preferable to Stage I. This is something that is important to remember as a coach. People evolve and develop throughout their lives and they will always have adaptations. It is not a question of simply good and bad, but a question of suitability. As a coach, if a person wants to improve their relationships but they do not take responsibility for their own feelings and thoughts (and see them 'out there' – projection) this may be an area that needs coaching. This cannot just be about changing voice tone or physical approach – it is something far deeper. The person needs to leap a level of consciousness and in turn disembed themselves from the previous level's adaptations.
This then, is what you can help people to do. This is Developmental Coaching.

To do this, the coach will need to gently reflect back at them how their own behaviour is at least partially responsible for the responses of another person, e.g. if the coachee doesn't see they are partly responsible because of drug abuse, blame, personal failure and procrastination etc. In turn, this will help the coachee increase their level of awareness to what they are doing and the implications of their actions. They will begin to put themselves in other people's shoes more often.

On a different note, this is an interesting stage of adaptation for the coach. These adaptations are actually quite commonplace in adults and it is worth exploring the left-over traits within ourselves, even if we don't count our own consciousness as wholly within the stage II class, because stage II manifestations may still arise once in a while (especially when the times get tough!) In short, if most people are operating at stage III adaptations, the self can still regress to stage II because the stage III self still has access to the earlier stages that served so well in earlier years. For example, under stressful circumstances, the self may find itself sliding down to lower stages of adaptation when the ones usually employed no longer function to hold the self together – this regression to lower stages may happen in stressful situations, but it can also happen when we are tired, hungry etc. Aside from this, if the coach comes across an individual who predominately employs these adaptations, there is a challenge for the coach because on the whole, these are not 'likeable' adults. This is the hard part about coaching, especially when considering that earlier I mentioned that a prerequisite for Developmental Coaching was to like the coachee. For those coaches who possess a high level of kindness, tolerance and compassion, I tip my hat to your perseverance with my one hand whilst pointing towards more reading materials with the other. I think that through understanding Vaillant and Carl Roger's work in particular, a coach can appreciate how best to help their coachee move on from this somewhat unsavoury stage.

Adaptations stage III

The word 'neurosis' has become commonplace in our culture and has some heavy associations. Even though the stage III adaptations are called 'neurotic', they are actually healthy adaptations to life for individuals aged three to ninety. This band of adaptations is the most common that you will come across and, even though they are seen as just quirky from the outside, they do restrict freedom of expression. As Daniel Goleman says in *Vital Lies, Simple Truths*, "we are piloted in part by an ingenious capacity to deceive ourselves, whereby we sink into obliviousness rather than facing threatening facts". This is true at all stages of adaptation.

In contrast to the stage II immature defences that were in relation to interpersonal conflict, stage III adaptations are internalised problems, i.e. intrapersonal. As these adaptations cause concern to the individual, they will often seek help to resolve them. There is good news for coaching as through the process of increasing awareness and appropriate interventions, it is straightforward to change them. As I have indicated, as a Developmental Coach one of the skills you need to develop is the ability to interpret the coachee's situation in ways that indicate their current level of development and adaptation. To develop this skill, you will need the adaptations spelling out within yourself and through personal exploration, with a few moments of 'ah, I do that!' before finding the same ways of coping (adaptating) in others. If the coach is happy to root around within themselves and seek suitable interventions to resolve a neurotic disorder, they too will be able to grow and develop. As you will see, it is bringing awareness to bear on them that makes a huge difference. The release of intrapsychic tension when a neurotic defence is no longer employed can feel liberating – its continuation can lead to obsession about our neurotic behaviours, i.e. neurosis about our neurosis. The stage III adaptations are briefly explained below.

Intellectualisation
This adaptation arises when an individual separates the thought from the feeling about a person or object, leaving a cold rationalisation in its place. So the thought 'I hate them' is present, but there is no feeling. This adaptation also includes obsessions created to avoid bringing real feelings to the surface.

Repression
Repression is when the idea has been lost, but the feeling remains. Interestingly, this process of 'forgetting' a problem often leaves the person doing something that points towards them 'not really forgetting' completely, i.e. the unconscious still provides pressure against the psyche.

Phobias
Somewhere between intellectualisation and repression lie phobias – when there is a strong physical reaction to a person or object.

While this is certainly a neurotic defence, I have placed it here because in phobias the original event is often lost or repressed. The person may even 'dissociate' from the pain completely so that there is no feeling left either. This can be done by 'blotting out' with alcohol or peak joyful experiences.

Displacement
This occurs when the individual's attention is shifted or 'displaced'. For example, if someone is concerned about intimacy with their partner, they may become obsessed with a toy aeroplane, a stamp collection or a body part. In other words, the real issue is avoided and attention moved elsewhere.
Neurotic denial occurs when someone simply denies that there is a problem to be dealt with, even though there clearly is.

Reaction formation
This adaptation arises when the individual's behaviour is the opposite to their unconscious desire. This may manifest as a reaction against a certain behaviour, such as eating chocolate, by 'stopping it dead'. This leads the person to feel the desire but they react against it with abstinence.

As an overview, what we have looked at above is the relationship between an idea and a feeling. This is another way of looking at it:
- intellectualisation there is the idea but no feeling
- repression there is feeling but no idea
- displacement of attention the feeling is associated with something else
- reaction formation the idea and feeling at a conscious and unconscious level don't match

For the Developmental Coach, this must be seen as just the beginning to understanding these mechanisms but this approach could be useful as an aide memoire, as the feeling moves around the place- sometimes connected, sometimes not.
To obtain a deeper appreciation of what your coachee is experiencing and the associated adaptive mechanisms they are using to cope with life, further self exploration will be needed but I will use case studies to help place your understandings. In the meantime use self-reflection and 'defence' spotting within yourself and you will start to get them on-board. When you turn your

analysis on yourself at this level, you will find that you almost certainly employ neurotic defences – this is perfectly normal and actually healthy. Even though they may cause you initial concern, I would encourage light heartedness as we all use adaptive mechanisms to deal with life and, even though stage IV may be preferable to stage III, most people at stage IV still employ these adaptations as well. The 'neurotic' adaptations are the most prevalent and not too major a problem from a psychoanalytic viewpoint, but for the individual using the defence, as soon as they become aware of what they are doing, they may well want to deal with it.

Methods of dealing with neurosis

The question arises about whether awareness is enough in most circumstances when people are working with this on their own. An individual may be aware of an obsession or a phobia but in this situation it is quite likely that they will not be able to shift it. However, as Developmental Coaching is neither about conventional therapy nor trying in some way to 'fix' a person, it is not your responsibility to attempt to remedy the situation. Instead, your responsibility is to support the individual's growth and development – it may well be that the neurosis is stopping the coachee's development at this stage and it can be of concern to you that this is being employed, but it is *not* your role to try to fix it. Even though on occasions it is darn tempting to have a go! You may well suggest that the coachee explores a therapy route if they want and as Vaillant says, "the user of neurotic defences is a self-diagnosed sinner who gratefully confesses and thereby wins absolution." Alternatively, you may point the coachee in the direction of suitable reading material. In some cases, increasing the coachee's awareness will bring together the 'idea' and the 'feeling' through discussion of what is going on, but this requires considerable skill on the coach's part. Many coaches have found that reading material (as a form of "bibliotherapy"- I like that word) has aided their coachee to move through the neurotic realms – by reading about a condition and applying what they have read, the coachee is able to 'see through' their patterns of behaviour and move on from that adaptation. It is through the conversational support of the coach that they are able to do so with confidence. However, this does not mean that the individual taking this route stops employing neurotic defences – on the contrary, they will find that many other neurosis are probably present, but they do not cause enough of a problem to require intense work in this area (yet). Note: If a coachee becomes an 'expert' on their neurosis but they have not shifted, a gentle nudge in the direction of a therapist may help them take that extra step.

In *Integral Psychology*, Wilber sums up how therapy works and I am suggesting that Developmental Coaching can have a similar affect as the coach becomes the 'catalyst'. Whereby the coach can "allow consciousness to encounter (or reencounter) facets of experience that were previously alienated, malformed, distorted or ignored." Wilber continues that the reasons this can cure is because "by experiencing these facets fully, consciousness can genuinely acknowledge these elements and thereby let go of them." Continuing with Wilber's perspective, this process allows for the growth or development of an individual to occur as the coachee is able to see these elements "as an object, and thus differentiate from them, de-embed from them, transcend them- and then integrate them into a more encompassing, compassionate embrace."

NOTE: The earliest adaptations of psychosis, splitting and narcissism are not dealt with best through reflection and integration into the existing ego structure (when serious). There is simply too little ego there in the first place. As the problem occurred when there was little ego present, the treatment is generally 'structure building'. This leads to sufficient ego to then continue with the development of it. Quality psychotherapy is still a suitable route with this in mind.

Optimal living

Overall, neurotic defences can cause the person to live a less than optimal life – a life filled with contradictory feelings, rampant obsessions and a high degree of personally restricted freedom. Trying to 'keep it all in' in the case of repression can lead someone to physiological problems as well as emotional concern. If the person is bubbling over with emotion, they are using heavy internal tactics (in a way that is what an adaptation is at an unconscious or conscious level) to avoid exploding when that final straw breaks the camel's back. In 'dissociation', the individual may totally cut off from the issue (not just from the idea) – in 'intellectualisation', they can be a little 'cold' as the feeling has been separated. In 'reaction formation', the person may be denying natural urges that could be enjoyed and explored if only the defence was not used.

But these defences are often not released easily. We need our defences. Our realities are operating at a level that requires defences to hold ourselves together. But from a Developmental Coaching perspective, we do not aim to delve into the past to make sense of who we are. A perspective of the past may well be useful, but from the *Grant Study* research, it really is the sustained relationships with people that moulds our character. The quality of life of the members of the study was determined by the level of adaptation they used. This was irrespective of their background, including economic situation and childhood. Looking back at the lines of development we discussed earlier and bringing it together with the defences present at different levels of consciousness – the neurotic level being 'what if?' and 'full what if?' – we see that people with more development over several lines will be more balanced as individuals. When this is combined with the 4 Quadrants and their activity in those quadrants, we can begin to see how an individual might live a more loving and fruitful life.

For the person developing through 'what if?' thinking (as is expressed through the neurotic adaptations), the next level will bring forth its own adaptations to life. The 'what what if?' level of thinking – vision logic, using Wilber's words, post formal operational/dialectical – has defences that are even more healthy and even an appreciation that they exist at this level can help spark an individual's interest in working through the neurotic defences. They do sound rather nice afterall. This may take some time, but it is through good quality relationships, for example with a coach, that the individual can exhaust the satisfaction gained at the neurotic defence level and move on to a higher order of self.

The most healthy adaptations to life are known as the 'mature defences' and are available to adults of any age. They are, however, considerably less common than the earlier stages of defence. Jane Loevinger in *Theories of Ego Development* says, "The striving to master, to integrate, to make sense of experience is not one ego function among many, but the essence of ego." And it is at this stage of development – 'what what if?' – that adaptations begin to reflect the coming together, or integration, of the ego. From an integral perspective, this is the level which holds much joy and freedom for those individuals fortunate enough to stabilise it. But this fortune comes not by chance, but through high quality relationships and committing to concentrated effort. This level is not closed off to any human; it is just a case of catching the next wave and releasing from the addiction of the previous status quo. I repeat, this is not a level that is open only to academics or scholars, or artists and musicians – this level and its adaptations are free for all. But before attaining this level, the self must find its way through the previous levels, find them ultimately unsatisfactory and then move on.

For many, the description of the adaptations will be seen as if they are simply 'good' qualities, or 'pleasant traits'. But they are also ways of coping with life – ways of adapting to experiences and in turn adapting those experiences back into life. For the Developmemtal Coach, these are qualities to be appreciated and maybe even sought after, but they are not just qualities. It is at this level of being that the self has begun to integrate itself into a form that is of a higher order.

The stage IV adaptations are briefly explained below.

Suppression
This adaptation is active when the individual postpones action until another time. 'I'll deal with this on Tuesday.' The individual does not then forget about it but chooses an appropriate time, and probably an appropriate state, to deal with a situation.

Anticipation

This mechanism allows the individual to prepare themselves for discomfort, such as surgery or loss. This conscious acceptance allows for realistic planning instead of avoidance.

Altruism and humour

Service towards others is a naturally emerging quality that provides a real benefit to the people who receive it. Humour allows a light hearted reflection on what may not be light hearted.

Sublimation

This is when energy is channelled towards, for instance team sports or artistic expression. Hobbies that are not employed to avoid reality, and maybe even give pleasure to a greater number of people, can be included here.

Even though these adaptations seem very 'normal' and positive, they are still ways of dealing with life. For example, the philanthropist who engages with good causes is actually adapting him or herself through the mechanism of altruism; the businessman who calmly deals with problems at an appropriate time with foresight of future consequences may be using suppression. But no matter what defences are employed, it is worth noting that the previous stages (all the way down to stage I) are still available to the individual. Because they have emerged through these stages, the individual still has access to them if the circumstances are right or, as it really is, when the circumstances are wrong. In particular, under stress the movement from Stage IV to Stage III is the easiest to occur. For many, the neurotic defences will still only be a button pressing experience away – when the button is pressed, regression to an earlier defence will occur. And if the movement to Stage III adaptations does not stabilise the situation, the individual may attempt to hold themselves together by slipping down the developmental spiral even further. When you add in that there are often remnants of the earlier stages still within the self (pathologies), the downward journey can happen quite quickly.

Comparison to neurotic defences

Mature defences often develop out of the continued use and failure of the neurotic defences (as in 'the translations fail'). Repression, as a neurotic defence, enables the individual using it to push away the idea that is of concern to them. For instance, in a relationship if someone has behaved in a certain way and it has led to a strong emotion, the problem itself may be avoided to avoid confrontation. Repression's natural successor is suppression, when the individual decides to face the discomfort at a suitable time. Instead of leaving the feelings to stack up, they may, using the same example, be talked through and the intrapsychic tension dissipated as a result. The process of suppression is thereby more mature, as the energy that would have been used in repression can be used elsewhere.

Similarly, instead of displacing attention (or dissociating from the issue altogether), someone at the mature stage may use anticipation to deal with problems. There is a high degree of honesty when a person does this as they have to face their own fears and troubles; they may also start to prepare for their inevitable demise – this is certainly not a stage that thinks it is immortal.

Altruism and/or humour can lead a person to be warmer and kinder in the eyes of others. But this is not its purpose as there is a high degree of satisfaction for the employer of this adaptation. Unlike wit, which uses displacement of attention, Vaillant says, humour enables the person to be inclusive and, instead of it being a distraction, it actually helps us face the unfaceable, whatever that may be. I personally went to stand-up college in San Francisco for 6 months to play with this idea. It really works! In a similar way, there is honesty in sublimation too – a person does not deny what they feel, but expresses it through a suitable medium. But Vaillant does not see that movement through adaptations up to this stage, and motion in life, is necessarily easy for the individual. "Anxiety and depression, like blisters and fractures, become the price of a venturesome life. In daring to live and grow up, we create disparities between conscience and instinct, and between that precarious balance and the people we love."

So, mature adaptations are not just 'good qualities' – they are real adaptations to life. This means they are naturally emergent within the personality when it reaches a certain level of maturity. Most commonly it is later in life that people stabilise this level, but it can occur much earlier if the circumstances are optimal. This is where Developmental Coaching can assist.

Adaptive versus intentional needs

Now that we have gone through the four stages of adaptations that occur at the different stages of development, the main focus needs to shift on to how this helps the Developmental Coach. As such, let us now return back to a central coaching principle - that of "goals". With a basis that coaching requires a good relationship with the coachee, it is necessary that this relationship develops over time so the coach can observe and assist in the development. But at every stage, the coachee will be moving on, standing still or moving backward. The reason that sits behind this is the adaptive mechanisms that the individual employs as they operate at a certain level of consciousness within the 4 quadrants of life – I, we, it and its – and with a focus on certain lines of development.

Adaptive mechanisms can hold people back just as much as a movement through them can move the person on. When we talk as a coach in terms of 'goals', there is a fundamental problem – the goal is itself a reflection of the coachee's intentional needs. They 'want' something. But wanting is not enough. If the adaptive mechanisms are not in place to support the intention, the coachee will be unable to achieve their goals. This is key for you as a coach. The adaptive needs need to be less than the intentional needs. In other words, if the person needs to be operating at a low level of adaptation, then this will override any intentional need they might have. For instance, if a person has not felt loved enough, they may behave in an unsuitably selfish way. In this case, the person may be operating at an immature defence level. If this person wants to be kindly towards others (maybe because their boss has told them, maybe because they feel they ought, or just because they simply would 'like to') then they may still be unable to so because their adaptation will override the intention. The adaptation serves as a way for them to deal with life, even if this may seem strange as an outsider.

You see how useful this session is now? It makes a huge difference to understanding the person you are coaching.

So, the individual's adaptive needs rule their actions. Even if a goal is set, it is by no means an indication that the person has the adaptive capacity to achieve it. For example, if someone wants to give up an obsession or a habit, this is a goal (an intentional need), but they can only achieve it if their adaptive need for the obsession or habit does not hold them back. Adaptive needs *always* override intentional needs.

As a coach, and bringing this together with the GROW model – Goal, Reality, Options, What next? – it is worthwhile considering the 'reality' aspect when the goal is set. If you see that the coachee's adaptive needs are likely to override their intention to satisfy the goal, you may want to assist in changing the goal while helping them gain experiences to evolve their adaptive needs. However, your role as Developmental Coach is not to destroy the coachee's dreams and long-term goals, but rather to support the coachee's development to a point where their goals are easily achievable in accordance with their adaptive needs. Hence, once again this type of coaching can be seen as using goals as a vehicle to aid the development of another human being.

From the results of following the lives of the men in the *Grant Study*, Vaillant saw that "over the course of a lifetime, styles of adaptation seem to have much more effect on outcome than the insults that chance inflicted upon the men." When Vaillant talks of outcome, he refers to a scale that considers success in career, relationships, health etc. The men with 'good outcomes' were using higher level adaptations than the men with 'bad outcomes'. This has to be useful to know as a coach! "One of the great lessons that I learned from these men – one of the real lessons to be derived from the prospective study of lifetimes – is the corollary finding that the sons-of-bitches in this world are neither born that way nor self-willed. Sons-of-bitches evolve by their unconscious efforts to adapt to what for them has proven an unreasonable world." It is this perspective that shows the importance of appreciating where a coachee is coming from. If someone is operating at a low stage of adaptation, condemnation will not help, but appreciation might. Maybe it won't be the sons-of-bitches that will be coachees (or coaches) but at least we can increase our tolerance through appreciation that what they are doing is trying to serve the purpose of adapting to life. This is what we are all doing, in our own way.

So progression through these stages of adaptation is most often a gradual and life-long process. As a coach you cannot rush the process, but you can certainly assist in the movement through the stages of adaptation. Vaillant says that "if defences cannot be taught, they can be absorbed". And the people we have around us are the most likely role models for us to absorb adaptations from. There is little we can do in respect of the mentors and teachers of our own upbringing, whether good or bad, but the opportunity now is to influence people through the medium of the more healthy adaptations. Even though we are talking about absorption rather than learning in a classroom, it is this type of learning that internalises the mentors and coaches that we all have. As Vaillant puts it, "If part of any talent depends upon good teachers, part of any talent comes from a continued capacity to learn and to synthesize what others teach."

When we can influence those around us, having stabilised a level of adaptation that allows the interests of others to override the need for ourselves during coaching, we can set the scene for absorption to occur. If ever there was 'walking the talk', this is it. It is at the adaptive level that real substance to character can be seen and the level at which it exists. This is key to our journey and to those we are coaching.

Questions for reflection (yes, quite a few):

Think of the most developed/successful people you know – which of these adaptations do they portray?
When do their adaptive needs override their intentional needs?
Which are you developing in yourself?
Which old adaptations will you let go of in favour of the mature adaptations?
What traits do you see as 'leftovers' in others, and even yourself?
When should you recommend a coachee seeing a therapist?
How can you support the coachee as a friend?

Considering that stage III adaptations are common, which are present in the behaviours of the coachee? How will you approach any ideas in a kindly manner?

Do these adaptations cause the coachee a problem – how will you help them transform them?

Are they surrounding themselves with people who are allowing lower adaptations to continue to be supported? Are there 'yes men' in their lives?

Notice how often these adaptations occur – how do you react as a coach – what about your feelings?

What can you do to help?

How will you help them move on?

Session 5
States, sub-personalities and the self

States, sub-personalities and the self

Do you recall how I said the last session was a long one? Well, session 5 could be a lot shorter in the written form. Having looked at how a person develops through the levels of consciousness with their associated adaptations, this session looks at the states, emotions and feelings that a person may have and how a coach can relate to them. It may sound "back to basics" for many a reader but as you are building a broader map, you may start to see them rather differently. I personally find by the fifth session myself and the coachee are rolling along well- the relationship is allowing the process to occur in a very natural fashion.

So to clarify and recap, the levels of consciousness can be seen as relatively stable 'structures' that tend to endure over time and then, if all goes well, evolve into higher order structures or levels. At each of these levels exists a series of ways for adapting to life. These adaptations are ways for the individual to manage themselves when they have a certain structure of consciousness. But what has not been considered are the states, emotions and feelings that may be present, and from that, what a person actually feels. These states are different to emotions, but it is from them that emotional states come. Some states can be described as background states such as an aching back, or a general pleasant state of the body. These can be exhilarated states as much as they could be depressed ones; bu if we enter into a more depressed state that lasts, we are going to find that our performance is reduced. Often, we don't return 'that important call', we don't persist at moving towards our goals, and we are generally not consistent in our efforts. On the other hand, it is when we enter states that are well motivated and focused that people have the most optimal states – there is a higher level of commitment and enthusiasm for the direction that the person has chosen. As the self is complex, there is not just one state that we reside in – the state can change dependent on circumstance. So, in this session we work with the coachee to make them more aware of the states they tend to be accessing day to day.

Interestingly, the personality often has many states within it that are at different levels of consciousness, and many are included within 'as if', 'what if?' and 'what what if?' In the same way that adaptations are related to levels of consciousness, states also have an intimate developmental relationship. This is important for the Developmental Coach, as the support offered to the coachee is more appropriately directed if the state of the coachee is understood – in other words, you need to know where they are coming from. Even though it is a temporary state rather than a level of consciousness/stage of development, the coach can help the individual move into a better state. So in the short term the coach can support the coachee and aid their movement within a level. In the longer term the coach will help the individual move between levels through the methods we have already discussed-"holding" them over time and using the techniques from earlier sessions. In the session itself it can be so powerful and so effective to get them to shift state. This is common throughout many coaching methodologies - the coach gets into a positive emotional state themselves and "drives" the state of the coachee. This can be done by accident as well. As it happens, when I am coaching (or generally chatting with people) I get highly energised. This tends to be infectious.

There are also particular states called "sub personalities" that can often hijack the self and reduce our competencies and abilities. This concept is something else for you to add into your coaching toolbox, especially when you relate it to this stage in Developmental Coaching. The coachee may well be ready to start looking at this principle even though it could be a little odd! These sub-personalities are states appearing as bits of the self at different levels and arise when the move through the developmental spiral is uneven, i.e. aspects of the self may be at a lower stage of development. If these are relatively cohesive states they will show up as sub personalities – facets of the person, but at a lower developmental stage. Makes sense? For instance, if a person falls into a 'miserable child state' that lasts for ten minutes, this is likely to be a sub personality. These lesser personalities can be from any level of consciousness and Wilber says they can be known as "parent ego state, child ego state, adult ego state, topdog, underdog, conscience, ego ideal, idealised ego, false self, authentic self, real self, harsh critic, superego, libidinous self, and so on." Assuming that there is no serious mental health problem (such as multiple personality disorder), then the movement into any of these states is quite natural. They come, hang around for a while and then go again. These sub personalities show up as "different vocal or subvocal voices in one's inner dialogue" and may also appear with certain associated feelings. For the coachee, however, they may find this gives them a feeling of being 'all over the place'. For them, the hijacking by one of these states may not make it easy for them to have the life they choose. As these mini-selves are at lower levels of consciousness, they also have the lower level adaptations as well. This can lead the coachee to behave in less than optimal ways when they are 'under the influence', i.e. instead of acting at their normal level of adaptation, they drift downwards, utilising the more primitive ways to cope. A person may have the ability to access 'what if?' thinking but actually be collapsing into states that are at the 'as if' or 'pre as if' level.

In the Developmental Coaching context, the idea of states can be seen a) a way of "jollying someone along, as I mentioned and b) more comprehensively as bringing together these parts of the self so the higher order (in this case the self at the 'what if?' level) is more consistent. Author and trainer Michael Hall's work on states and meta-states is a lovely guide to this realm and deals specifically with how changing the way we relate to our states can improve our lives. Check it out for his views as well.

Working with states

If there is something we consider to be a normal 'self', then the sub personalities are pilots that take over at the wheel temporarily – it may be a temper tantrum, a patch of low self-esteem or a feeling of superiority that invades into consciousness for a time before falling back into the depths once more. From the outside, this may seem strange as the person could move through quite an array of states with relative fluidity. From the inside, and without an appreciation of what is happening, this fluidity may make the individual feel like this is perfectly normal – it's 'just how they are'.

Despite saying that this is a normal phenomenon, it may be that it causes concern to the coachee. If so, and seeing Developmental Coaching as a vehicle to doing so, the coachee can "bring awareness to bear on these sub personalities, thus objectifying them, and thus including them in a more compassionate embrace" (Wilber). In the same way as dealing with releasing the grip of certain neurotic adaptations, the coachee can see through the sub personality and in this process can 'have it' instead of 'being had by it'. This way, and over time, the sub personality will be integrated into a more complete sense of self, and the personality come from a more stable centre rather than shifting from state to state. As this requires the coachee to 'see through', it is a degree of self-reflective consciousness that is likely to need at least 'what if?' thinking, but more likely 'full what if?' thinking. In other words, they need to make the leap to self-authoring their world. This is when the individual can objectify their internal world of feelings and emotions. Through the process of integrating the sub personalities, the person is encouraging this move into 'full what if?' thinking. In this way, the coach can aid the coachee transform their level of consciousness. This has been my own experience with many clients and has usually made a significant difference to their lives.

The process one undergoes to integrate these 'bits of the self' is relatively straightforward for the coachee. By noticing that they have drifted into a sub personality, they have already taken awareness beyond the act of being in that sub personality state. This means that the person is no longer just in the state, but aware that they are in the state. This is a 'meta' position to that state whereby the person has gone beyond the state and made it into an object. The self that then sees the state as something other than him or herself is freed from acting as if in that state. It is this observation and non acting that allows the integration process to occur. The energy of the sub personality is dissipated as the individual notices and remains noticing instead of acting them out. You will find early stages of many meditative techniques will encourage this process, especially those focused on concentration practices whereby the individual dis-embeds themselves and "sits back" as an observer to those mental objects. Once they can sit with a degree of comfort without getting "caught up in it all" then they can begin to simply be aware of what is happening.

As coach you may choose to encourage this reflection process. As the coachee observes without action, they will see, hear and feel what is occurring in their mind. This witnessing process greatly aids everything being 'bought together'. It might, however, be a challenge to witness in this way as it requires the ability to disembed from the workings of one's mind (a 'full what if?' function). If so, the coachee might find that a form of formal concentration practice to steady their ability to concentrate (this could be focus on the breath, or counting without losing the thread) will help focus the mind. I hasten to add that this is not really meditation (but has similarities with very early stages of meditation practice), but is just a way for the coachee to 'see through' more easily. The ability to concentrate without being absorbed into these states is an indication that they are being integrated. It is even likely that it will become a game for the coachee who is able to spot the sub personalities in themselves as there is considerable freedom associated with the process of integration. Over time this non-action will lead to them being greatly freed; and it will also lead to a more integral feeling. However, if a person continues to find they drift into the states, i.e. the states hijack them, then more concentration practice is needed.

Feelings and emotions

Emotions, in contrast to feelings, are 'displayed'. This means that from the outside a person can see that they are in a certain emotional state. This is done as both a voluntary and involuntary response, and includes the emotional states of happiness, joy, frustration, confusion, indifference, excitement, anger, boredom, curiosity, bliss etc.

In coaching we often look at supporting someone through a certain challenge and this support is actually a support for the way the person is feeling. When there is trust in a relationship, a person will open up 'how they feel'. This opening up about their feelings is quite different to the emotional response and outward display of that emotion. The feeling may describe a bodily state, such as 'I feel a discomfort in my leg' or 'I feel an ache in my head' or a mental representation 'I feel light'. This is much more an indication of what is happening internally for the coachee, i.e. they have a location in the body (in the chest, abdomen etc) and will vary in intensity. Sometimes, when these feelings have been pushed away, it will be necessary to reconnect to these feelings and bring the mind and body together once more (as mentioned in healing the mind-body split).

If the coachee can describe feelings of pleasure and pain to you, the relationship takes on new meaning – they are sharing the intimacy of their subjective experience, not just showing an outward sign. You can choose to share how you feel too; and it is this reciprocation that aids the deepening of the relationship. Further, when the coachee is able to know the feeling, they can create space around it. This creation of space (as we have mentioned) leads to the feelings being made objects, or putting it simply, they become something other than 'I'. When a person can talk about their inner experience and how they 'feel' about, let's say, a goal, it will help determine whether they are likely to achieve, or stop themselves achieving it.

In terms of application areas, you will have experienced asking someone 'How are you?' and had them give the polite response of 'I am fine.' But this is often not the case. This default response can be hiding away feelings that would be better recognised. 'How do you feel?' will point a coachee in the direction of their internal experience. And it is through the acknowledgement and working through of feelings that they can best integrate their experiences.

An example of a health problem is when the coachee does not look at their feelings but represses them instead. If these feelings are left unaccepted, they can turn against the body's immune system and in time cause ill health.

Furthermore, by understanding that sub-personalities may well 'run the show' for short periods, we can see that rash judgements may well be taken during these periods. In a business context, a sub personality that is determined to be the underdog may well mean the business 'will never work', merely in order to satisfy that sub personality. If a coach can notice that even when the business is going well, a member of the team is determined to satisfy the needs of this sub personality, then appropriate action can be taken. Helping the coachee see through their sub personality (and maybe the coachee catching themselves just about to enter into this state) and focus on satisfying the more inclusive and greater encompassing needs of the rest of the personality may help them abate the sub personality's affect.

If a person can integrate their sub personalities, it can have a positive affect on relationships. Sub personalities are often triggered because they have associated circumstances, such as a dispute with a partner. If the coachee is unaware of the sub personality, the pattern of behaviour is likely to continue. If the coach brings the awareness of sub personalities to the coachee's attention (maybe through reading), the coachee may begin to see how the sub personality plays a key part in the interaction going the way it does and in time, the coachee may choose to integrate this part of themselves, thereby freeing themselves from that old response.

The self

So far we have discussed Developmental Coaching in relation to many different areas, including lines of development, levels of development and adaptations, and states (including sub personalities). What has not fully been recognised is the thing that binds these all together. Who is actually going on this developmental journey? There is a 'self' that moves through the lines and levels and experiences the states. This self is very much what you call 'you'. The self is responsible for taking the leaps and for releasing from earlier developmental stages; it is a determining factor in achieving a certain level of performance; it brings together experience so it can be integrated; it utilises its defences to stabilise a level. In other words, the self is a kind of navigator that keeps everything flowing, and it is this self that we focus on next. I find that this allows the coachee during this session to "grasp" a little more and regularly I see a light bulb appear at this point. I like to reassure them that, in terms of the main theory of Developmental Coaching we are well on the way there! That let's them know much of the theory, at least, has been covered and now it is about the self putting it all to good use. There is still a little more, of course, we do have two more sessions to go through, but as I say, it is good to let them know how far we have come.

So now we will run through six characteristics of the self:

Identification

This is what a person considers to be 'I' as opposed to 'me'.

Most people consider what they are in terms of their occupation or role, e.g. a manager, therapist, mother, father etc. These you would call 'me'. But there is a sense of self that observes this called 'I'. This 'I' is the subject, and the 'me' aspects are objects – there is a seer (I) and there is the seen (me).

Organisation
Wilber says in Transformations of Consciousness that the self 'gives (or attempts to give) unity to the mind', in other words it 'organises'.

Will
The self has the ability to choose its options. However, these options are present only at the self's current level of consciousness. For instance, the self cannot choose to form hypotheses (what if? thinking) if is only operating at 'as if?'. The individual's choices, options and free will are limited by this.

Defence
The adaptations and defences are within the self. (Coachees often find this reassuring as they can fit the pieces together even more.)

Metabolism
Experiences are metabolised (or digested) by the self.
For instance, if experiences were food, then when a past experience is not fully metabolised and integrated, they will tend to give heartburn. This shows up as 'bits of the self' that exist at a lower level, and includes sub personalities. (Again, coachees often go...'Ahhh!')

Navigation
The self is responsible for 'letting go' or 'holding on to' the individual's current level. It is through the letting go process that the self can move on.

As the self moves through the levels, it is dis-identifying with the previous level – what it considered to be 'I' at one level becomes 'me' at the next. So there is a 'movement over' from the subject (I) to it being an object (me). Understanding this helps us to identify how 'seeing through' what we once were, frees us from it. In relation to some of the adaptations and sub-personalities, this process of the 'I' subsequently being seen as the 'me' is the essence of human development. Relating it back to the levels of consciousness ('as if', 'what if?', 'full what if' and 'what what if?') at each stage this process is occurring – the self moves into an object position (i.e. it can be seen as 'other' than itself) what it previously identified with *being itself*. As coach, aiding this 'seeing' or 'witnessing' process of each stage, instead of the coachee acting within that stage, will help them move on. For instance, if a person can reflect on their thoughts, feelings and emotions, this is a movement towards a 'full what if?' level and away from the previous 'what if?' level where these thoughts and feelings made up the person's self. If someone no longer just operates in several contexts, but begins to find a relationship between the contexts, there is a movement towards 'what what if?' thinking (i.e. dialectical). So, what we were previously identified with at the previous stage becomes seen as something other than ourselves.

The self-structure also gives rise to the self sense that determines our internal conceptions of competency. People that consider they are 'good' or 'bad' at certain skills are driven to perform accordingly. This relates back to the earlier session. I use this to remind people not to forget about competencies even though we are taking a lot of time to discuss development.

Overall, if experiences are metabolised well, it will help to increase the unity of mind – if the experiences are not metabolised and integrated, the personality can be fractious. From a coaching perspective, the aim is to bring together the personality into a more stable self that is capable of navigating life without being held back. This principle of a freedom to navigate is essential to grasp. If the coachee is burdened by less than optimal adaptations (such as Stage II's immature defences) and less than healthy self-images, it is likely their life will be hugely challenging. This is because their defences are likely to override their 'will' element and as a result, the options realistically open to them will be limited, i.e. the intentional needs will be overridden by the adaptive needs, as discussed. For a coach, seeing the development of this picture of the coachee and of where they are at, you can decide how best to assist.

In the book so far, I have been laying the foundations of Developmental Coaching. It has been my intention to give an overview of the most essential aspects of the theory, but orienting it towards coaching as much as possible. The next sessions will have a strong focus on application, so if you are after tangible "skills" for your sessions then that should well do the trick. In real terms, with the coachee, I find this session will enable deeper conversations about "themselves". You will have truly built the relationship as well as looking at the theory and how to use the models. They will tell you their "real feelings" about their goals and you will be able to broaden your horizons as the navigator opens up more of their inner worlds.

Questions for reflection
How consistent is the coachee?
Will you, and should you, help the coachee become more integrated?
When do your own states and sub-personalities come into play?
What life experiences remain un-metabolised? Is the coachee turning any emotion against themselves?
Does the coachee repeat any pattern(s) of behaviour that are semi-fixed in the self? If appropriate, how will you offer support to make them aware of the issues?
Who does the coachee see themselves to be?

Session 6

Supporting the integral personality

Supporting the integral personality

As you will probably have started to see, there is a driving force towards integration within this coaching model. As the coachee starts to "pick up" and integrate all of those bits of themselves they left at earlier stages, as they reflect upon the workings of their internal world, they are becoming more integrated as a person. So by the time we get to this session, whilst knowing that all adaptations are still available to us, we tend to have a coachee who is seeking greater stability at those higher levels. At least, they will now be thinking about reflecting upon their internal worlds and "having feeling" instead of being "had by them" (i.e. self-authoring). It is this pivotal leap, I would suggest 50% of coaching clients tend to make great strides towards. I didn't want to tell you earlier as everything else is also really important! But there you have it. So let us now look at the more integral personality that is emerging.

Warren Bennis wrote in relation to organisational integrity, "The integral personality...I am talking about a kind of unity – of purpose, goals, ideas and communication – that makes three musketeers, Three Musketeers. It's a merging of identities and resolves into a coherent and effective whole.' If you had to sum it up then, this could well be the higher aim as a Developmental Coach. In other words, maybe it is to bring an individual through the process of learning and development to a point where they are integrated. With all the usual fractions of the perfectly normal personality, this may take some time, but it is time well spent. Integration will manifest in the realms of the mind, behaviour and the individual's operation within the cultural and social domains. It covers all areas of their life and for you as a coach, to aid the growth of another human being must be the one of the greatest gifts of the post-modern world.

So what will it look like? In *Experiential learning*, David Kolb says, "...integrity is a sophisticated integrated process of learning, of knowing. It is not primarily a set of character traits such as honesty, consistency, or morality.' In the same way that Vaillant discussed the higher level of adaptations, the mature mechanisms, Kolb sees that something emerges at a higher stage of ego

115

development. When someone becomes an 'integral person', their integrity has come about through a 'learning process by which intellectual, moral and ethical standards are created.' In Kolb's view, the 'pinnacle of development is integrity. It is that highest level of functioning that we strive for consciously and even unconsciously, perhaps automatically, to reach'. Abraham Maslow's hierarchy of needs is a well-known model that suggests that there are different requirements, i.e. needs, at different levels. When one level is satisfied, the next level of needs emerge. The movement from the needs that keep us alive, such as food and water, develops into the needs of safety and shelter. From there the need to 'belong' emerges, and then comes the requirements of self-esteem, initially gained from others and later generated within ourselves. The final stage in Maslow's model is that of self-actualisation. This is what we are really talking about for Developmental Coaching at the highest stages. For you as the coach it will be about considering the individual's needs and whether they are currently following an appropriate route to satisfy them. In one coaching case I remember, the coachee indicated they were seeking to self-actualise when in fact they hadn't satisfied their lower level needs. When they eventually focused on dealing with the adaptations that were holding them back, and over time, the coachee managed to satisfy their lower level needs such as having a stable job, a place to live and good relationships. The higher levels may seem more appealing, but in fact they are only available as a natural consequence of the self moving through the other levels. As Wilber says in *Sex, Ecology and Spirituality*, "you first have to have molecules, then cells, then organs, then complex organisms – they don't all burst on the scene simultaneously...the growth occurs in stages." He continues, "The more holistic patterns appear later in development because they have to await the emergence of the parts that they will then integrate or unify, just as whole sentences emerge only after whole words."

With different needs emerging at different levels we can see that by having a more complete view of the coachee's development, including their level of consciousness, adaptations and needs; the coach can identify much better where the coachee 'is at'. This in turn allows the coach to choose an appropriate approach for that stage. For the coachee the stages of needs are built on the previous stage, not negated by it. In the same way that a cell needs molecules to exist, a coachee must still have their basic needs satisfied after moving to a higher level of need – an individual cannot live on self-esteem alone! If at any stage a coachee becomes fixated by a wanting to be at a higher stage, then the coach's role is to gently firm up the foundations to allow them to achieve that level over time. Most often when the more fundamental needs are met there is a sense of relief for the coachee as the restriction will also be released. If, for instance, the coachee was seeking Enlightenment, but can't pay the bills, they will find enormous freedom from reacting against materiality when they begin to embrace it (even just a little). In a different case the coachee may be seeking the approval of others (a 'what if?' stage need as people are still dependant on others for their own identity) and find that they are having difficulty moving on. The coach may help them find ways to develop beyond this need in the ways we have already discussed. It is when the translations fail, 'I've tried everything', that the transformation can occur.

Here is a question that occasionally will come up: with one of the aims being the development of the coachee to ever higher stages, does the coach themselves have to be integral, or have an integral personality, to start with? In short, the answer is yes *and* no. Yes, it is preferable that the tour guide knows the environment; but no, the coach too is developing through the process of their coaching. Just like the example of the car and the road influencing each other when talking about a dialectical process, the coach and their coachees develop together. It is certainly unnecessary for the potential coach to hold off coaching until a point that they consider themselves to be integral – as long as they have an integral view, they can develop themselves to have an integral way of being. The integral personality is not that common, but it could be. Part of the purpose of this section is to show more signs of the integrated self, the integral personality. But Developmental Coaching is a set of principles that can be applied by anyone at any level of being. Someone at a 'what if?' stage can still be living an integral life, working to advance their lines of development within the four domains of life (see session 7) without being at a 'what what if?' stage, where the integrated personality is likely to truly emerge. In the same way, the Integral Coach can coach with an integral view, including the four domains (4 Quadrants), levels of consciousness, adaptations etc, and still be working towards being integral themselves.

There are several elements that can be brought together to show what it means to be this integral personality. This should prove useful when you have clients ready for this discussion. These factors include self-direction, cognitive complexity in relationships, pro-activity and rich life structures. The ability to be the author of one's life story, not just the passive recipient to it is essential as an emergent quality. It is quite likely that this will begin at the 'full what if?' level (full formal operational) but become fully 'real' as the personality becomes consolidated at an integral level. There is also the "increasing complexity in one's conception of personal relationships" – their relationship with the world is, Kolb continues, "transactional, in that they are proactive in the creation of their life tasks and situations and are shaped and molded by these situations as well". He also sees that the life structures mirror the complexity of the integrated personality. There is a greater amount of spontaneity in the life of the integrated personality as they are less bound within themselves to follow the normal constructs of day-to-day living. Interestingly, they experience less stress than those without an integrated personality despite their complex lives.

Looking at this another way, the integrated personality is able to bring together what Kolb calls the four learning styles. Kolb talks of two modes of grasping experience – one is through direct experience, concrete experience, and the other is through "symbolic representations of the experience", i.e. abstract conceptualisation. The first is grasping through doing, the second is grasping through building an internal model of experience. Kolb also talks of two modes of transforming. The first is through intentional reflection and the other through extensional action. I know what you are thinking? How the heck do I use this?! Well, from this we can see that we as individuals tend to favour one style of thinking – concrete, reflective, abstract or active i.e. one of these four. Yet it is the flexibility to move between styles that increases as the personality becomes more integral. We have already suggested that one way of seeing 'integral' is in the individual's movement to higher levels of development (across more lines) and using higher level adaptations while bringing together the parts of the personality. Re-read the paragraph above once again and you will see: you can grasp through doing/model building and you can transform through reflection/action. Flexibility of thinking, doing and being is all crucially important. So when you are coaching you want to consider what the coachee is actually doing/being/thinking with all the approaches and models with which you are working.

Communication

This session I like to also focus on communication with others. Some of what I will say will sound very basic indeed but we will come onto some case studies later. Sometimes we need to remember so much of coaching is about appropriate communication. First we will use the example of you, as the coach, yourself to start building the scene. We know a coach needs to be a good listener. It is when the coach notices not just the coachee's 'surface' replies/comments but looks at the deeper structure, they will reach further into the coachee's world. The coach's ability to notice subtle shifts in the coachee's language use, voice tone and body language will determine how effectively they can react in a one-to-one situation. Alongside the coach's ideas about the coachee's internal structure (built up through the methods in this book and all the other approaches they have learned as well), moment to moment the coachee will also display to the world what is happening through their verbal and non verbal communication. In one coaching situation, a very subtle unconscious twitch of a muscle to the side of the coachee's eye prompted me to ask, 'There seems to be some concern in going for that goal. If there was, what would it be?' This encouraged the coachee to voice their hidden concerns. From here I was able to encourage, 'hold' and support the coachee as they began exploring how a negative feeling about approaching a senior at work would hold them back. This acuity was supported by the coachee knowing that their adaptive needs were likely to hold them back in that situation. They would rather have repressed and denied the issue even though there was desire to deal with the situation. The ability to spot such subtle leakages of our internal thoughts and feelings can make a coaching session go far smoother than if they are missed.

As an example, in one coaching situation, I remember the coachee was feeling very tired and run down. This can happen; life is life. As the coach I had to understand this first. There is no point forcing someone into a positive state of mind when they think they have good reason to be in that state Instead, it was through changing my usual voice tone, which tends to be a little authoritative (well, I have my moments), to a softer tone that stepped in time to where the coachee 'was at'. This shift in tone helped the other person to be 'OK' where they were at. They had been concerned that the coach would try to 'jolly them up' and this at the time was not wanted. Over the course of an hour the unobtrusive approach was able to quietly move the coachee's state into a better one. This in turn led to the coachee actually shifted their body language and voice tone in a way that picked up the pace of the dance. In effect it was a simultaneous change both myself and the coachee reciprocated in the relational exchange. This "motion" in the situation came from understanding and support that allowed the coachee to take a movement on. Body language in a coaching context needs only a few words – be mindful of other's reactions to you and change yourself accordingly. This is how you must display your congruence and authenticity externally.

In a similar way the coach may choose to use the language that the coachee uses when describing their current, past or future situations. When the coachee feels understood they will open up more; when they feel misunderstood they will close down. Getting someone's language wrong is a great way to blow a relationship but getting it right often goes unnoticed. In one coaching exercise I used in a training, people were asked to differentiate three words. In the coachee's world these three words had different meanings; to the coach they had the same meaning. One coach found that even though they saw 'organisation, business and consultancy' as falling under the same banner of 'business', the coachee had a very different meaning for each one. The most important aspect of their organisation was "human resources"; most important for the business was profit and loss; and most important for the consultancy practice were the consultants' skills. This seemingly subtle differentiation that people have in their own worlds (created with its own language) must be respected and appreciated for the exchanges to go as smoothly as possible.

On a different language note, once the relationship has developed to a suitable point, the coach may choose to drop in slightly more technical language, such as lines of development, as this might get the coachee's interest and recommended reading may then follow. It is this ability to gently open the coachee to understanding themselves even better that will gain generative results in the coaching relationship. The coachee may move on and bring the coach a great richness of understanding, or they may begin to coach others as they learn explicitly how the coach had been thinking about their development.

I often find this session, if not Session 5, is the time to add in some additional skills. So, in a way, you want to be aware of all the existing ones you have in your toolbox, especially in relation to communication skills. People have truly started to "know themselves better" and it can be very handy for them to have some new approaches to play with. I tend to include Paul Ekman's work on micro-expressions - coachees tend to love this as they feel they have accessed a great hall of wizardry! Also, frame setting (including pre-frames, reframes and out-frames) and much NLP language (such as Meta and Milton patterns) find their merry way as well. These areas are well documented in many other books so I will let you explore which ones you feel would be useful for a coachee to receive at this point. When they experience a tangible difference in e.g. managing the context of a situation instead of having someone manage it (using frame setting) they will get a boost that the hard work is paying off.

Feedback and relational exchanges

At this point we must spend a few moments looking at the role of feedback both in relation to this model as well as in a coaching or business context. This is something, at some point, you are bound to be asked about as in our culture people have become quite used to 'giving other people feedback' as if it is something helpful to do. In the narrow remit of appropriate and inappropriate behaviour and in task-focused situations it can be useful, but in many other situations it is not. The brain is not a 'feedback friendly' organ, or rather instead of there being a 'looping' function between the neurology in the brain (where information is received and integrated), there is only a one way flow. In most cases the individual cannot actually do anything with feedback they receive. It is the neuron's 'looping' ability, or ability to integrate, that turns what would otherwise be feedback into something that the individual can work with. Furthermore, the neurology of some individuals is constructed in a way that prevents the necessary exchange occurring, so giving of feedback would be a waste of time. In the same way (for those that know Spiral Dynamics), giving feedback when someone is at 'red' (con-op) is taken as a very real threat to their sense of self. In fact, it can be damaging to all parties especially if individuals scurrilously give feedback to each other like, 'My feedback to you is that you didn't design that brochure to a high enough standard' and a response of 'You never give me the money I need to design it better.' Both are feedback, but it won't help the relationship. This 'feedback to feedback' approach is likely to 'get people's backs up' (or fire off people's lower stage adaptations) and is not an exchange – it is actually uni-directional, uni-directional from both sides. And it is when the feedback from life hits into your own concerns and pathologies, it will actually hold you back.. With an exchange (or using the neurological term of Edeleman, 're-entry') the person can take the information and adapt themselves with it. It is then they can move on.

I mention this because feedback for most people is not useful (outside the specified contexts) and, in coaching in particular, it can be useless at best and lead to many relational problems at worst. So, in terms of communication, as we are discussing in this section of this session, you may want to discuss this principle with the coachee. People resist feedback!

Case studies:
Below are some case studies that shine light on how communication is essential for individuals to understand at a deeper level.

In Jenny's case, I found out the importance of respecting and understanding someone's own internal world. It was a quiet reminder that we all have our own idiosyncrasies that come from our uniquely-wired neurology and resultant mind. Jenny was working as a personal assistant when she finally decided that she had had enough of the restriction on her life. The phobia that she had had from a very young age was leading her to become increasingly neurotic at work as well as home. She would make a joke out of it, but searching for spiders in her bed every night was no longer how she wanted to live. She decided to seek help. But the change in her life that is worth mentioning is not what you may think. Curing the phobia was less interesting than a comment she made in a later coaching session when she related the story of her meeting with the therapist. She explained that as she was asked by a therapist what happened when she heard the word 'spider', she cringed and her stomach 'turned'. The therapist then asked whether she had any positive associations with the same word. Instantly she said 'no', but then she smiled and said that it was actually her brother's nickname as a child. It was a day or so later (and now recalling the wonderful associations of her brother and her own childhood together when 'spider' is ever mentioned) she was doing a crossword. In a coaching session she explained thinking through a clue, asking for a gemstone that is 5 letters. She went through emerald, diamond... and then thought 'topaz, yes'. 'Why', she thought, 'do such beautiful things have such beautiful names – and nasty things have nasty names?' It didn't take her long to realise that we construct our meaning through our language and that the names themselves are just the juxtaposition of letters. As the coach I glimpsed a clear view of the importance of language in our communications. It is not the language in its own right, it is the meaning that is associated with it for an individual.

The next two case studies are contrasts.

The first situation was when Ben decided to show his book idea to a friend. She responded with great enthusiasm and encouraged him to send it to an agent who she was in close contact with. The agent, however, was less enthusiastic and rejected the idea. This was the first blow to his confidence, but the second fateful blow came from his friend's husband when he said, 'It is clear you cannot write.' As all parties in this case were held in high esteem by Ben, he took it to heart and put the manuscript back into the bottom drawer. But that was not all, sadly, he also put his emerging dream of being a writer in that drawer at the same time. In contrast, when one coachee was deciding whether to follow the 'bottom drawer route' for his own books, his coach said, 'You must keep on writing. Just get it out, keep studying and you will get there. You have a gift – all writers do.' The 'it' he spoke of was an array of varying books from self help through to business and the affect on the coachee was to feel the blind faith in himself may not be quite so blind after all. A few carefully chosen words from a respected person who has the necessary authenticity can turn a person's life around. In the first case, Ben took to heart the opinions of two people – one of which was not a writer – and Ben's new coach is aiding him moving on from his old beliefs. In the second case, the coachee was myself.

Modes of support

This next section is ideally placed in one of these later sessions and is especially useful when the motivation to achieve life's goals has been lacking or undermined. What many coachees really want is the support and motivation of a good coach. And there you are.
They want to feel there is someone waiting on the sideline, feel there is a friendly voice down the phone and be able to relate about the human experience and what it is to be a person. When someone starts feeling a lack of confidence they may start retreating from their goals, or only make a half hearted attempt to achieve them. When their results are not as good as hoped, the person's confidence can be even more undermined. On an internal level, the less mature responses will then tend to surface, and the coachee will tend to feel unsupported by life itself. Under these circumstances, the job of the coach in relation to motivation is to encourage and praise, often in an understated way, even the smallest of achievements. If the coach can break the negative circle of confidence leading to poor results leading to reasons to support low confidence, they can assist the coach to move on. If the coach is respected by the coachee, even a few words pointing them in the right direction can make all the difference – as coach, do not underestimate the potency of your role.

It is because the role is so important that makes a high degree of consistency of character, approach and content essential. When the coach can show the coachee consistency in these areas, they will feel supported even more. This is no truer than in the area of emotions. If the coach stabilises themselves, they can influence the

124

emotional state of the coachee. This can help to move someone from, for instance, a de-motivated way of being to a motivated way of being. Another influence the coach can have is to help the coachee to find their passion. This can be tied into their life plan and purpose, but is more to do with the one or two things that give them a glint in their eye when they talk about it. Nothing will motivate more than the chance to actualise one's dreams. The question now turns to what is the nature of the goal and what support do they need to get them there.

As we discussed earlier, competency is governed both by ability and the perception of ability (now and in the future). Due to the internalised view of their competency, "people tend to avoid activities and situations they believe exceed their coping capabilities, but they readily undertake challenging activities and pick social environments they judge themselves capable of handling" says Albert Bandura. Essentially we need to consider the interplay of challenge and support – people grow best when they experience sufficient challenge alongside an appropriate amount of support. The support model can be used to reflect whether aspects of someone's life are lived in a way to give the best opportunity for growth and development:

High challenge

1 Scary – can become defensive/ development hostile	**2** The right balance for development

Low support **High support**

3 Dull and boring – no growth	**4** Comfortable and easy – no growth

Low challenge

Looking at each box in turn you can see that there is an effect on a person's experience of the situation:

1 is when the person is out of their depth.

3 arises when the challenge does not stretch the person – they become bored.

4 the person may feel temporarily 'comfortable', but they are not developing.

2 is the only area where the person has true potential for growth, whether it is in a sport, a hobby, the work environment etc. Here the person can experience the urge to push themselves that little bit further because they have confidence that there are support structures in place. For example, a sports coach encourages sportspeople to perform within their full limits – the coach's skill is to know what conditions are needed to deliver the balance between challenge and support. The same applies in the workplace – if a mentor who knows the job well aims to help an individual, they will allow the individual to grow with the level of task that is required of them. As we mentioned earlier, they need to consider both the external and the internal factors. The question for both the individual and the coach becomes, 'How can we help adjust the person's internal conceptions of self and aid in performance enhancement?' Psychologist Bandura points to four main ways:

Most effective is success
It is the 'mastery experiences' in performance that build a strong sense of ability. Failure creates doubts. Even when there are setbacks, this strong self-certainty will help create perseverance which can, in turn, create positive performance.

The second method is by modelling
It is when we see people around us succeed that we can often feel inspired and interested. From these people we can also learn skills. Negative modelling can have the opposite effect.

Social persuasion
Social persuasion can be seen as coaches, mentors or skilled practitioners. As Bandura says, these people "do more than simply convey positive appraisals. In addition to cultivating people's beliefs in their capabilities, they structure situations for them in ways that bring success and avoid placing them prematurely in situations where they are likely to experience repeated failure."

Enhancing the individual's physical status and reducing stress levels
People often read their bodily states of stress as undermining their performance. Changing the individual's stress level will alter

their perception of their potential competencies and actual competencies.

When it comes to support, the balance must be right. While the role of the Developmental Coach may be to assist in helping all four of these areas come into fruition, overly supporting the individual with unnecessary help can cause them to lose their sense of competence, i.e. competence can easily turn into incompetence if the conditions are not optimal. For example, if a highly skilled person is put in a role that has an inferior label, they will find it more challenging to perform to their usual skill level. Similarly, competition can also affect performance. This is clear in the realm of sport where belief about another's competency can lead to psychological games as well as physical ones (and of course, they are not separate). If an individual expects a difficulty, they are more likely to perform less optimally.

Types of support

The method of support depends largely on the activity. As a Developmental Coach, you do not have to support every area of a coachee's life, but you might support them in gaining the support they need. For example, if the coachee is:
an active sportsperson, you may be able to support them in finding a sports coach to develop their innate talent
developing good business acumen, you might point them towards a course of study that could take this further
So the role of the Developmental Coach is not to be all things to all men, but the very fact that the approach is integral means that it will not necessarily exclude any area of the coachee's life.
Looking at the lines of development I have chosen, support may come in many different forms. The idea is to get you thinking about what else needs to be in place for the coachee to achieve their goals and dreams.

Cognitive
This includes the ability to 'grasp' within the areas of mathematical thinking, logic, reasoning etc, so support could be to direct the coachee to a good teacher, good books, courses etc.

Affect (emotional)
This relates to how the individual feels, including their feeling about other people's perceptions of them. For example, a group of friends or a business that stretches the individual can change the way the person feels about themselves and the way they feel about other's perception of them.

Interpersonal skills
This relates to relationships with others (which together with affect are similar to 'emotional intelligence'). People can achieve support through mentors, teachers, friends etc that helps them develop their relationships to greater depth.

Financial
This relates to abilities to provide for one's needs. Bank managers, advisors, books, achiever friends etc can provide assistance to develop this line.

Worldview
This is the appreciation of the difference between cultural perceptions. Reading about the dynamic changes in developing countries, culture and religion assist understanding and development. This is a huge area of potential study and can really push the developmental boundaries. If you take on Buddhist practice for instance, you may learn more about a Tibetan worldview - rather different to that in the West.

Meditative awareness
This is the practice of concentration and awareness practices. A community and teachers are especially useful (if not essential) in developing meditative awareness. With support structures in place you will be able to move on in the practice at a good rate; many don't ever really undertake meditation as they don't have proper instructions. Expert support here will make the difference.

Natural talent and ability
This may include linguistic capability, musical talent etc. People usually need a mentor or coach to take a natural ability further.

Physiological development
This is sporting ability, physical awareness etc which can be aided through a coach, teacher etc. For instance, for safety it is important to develop a sport with someone who has a high degree of skill beyond the individual's own.

Moral development
This includes a person's level of concern for others. Spending time with people who have a high level of care is support for developing this line. Increasingly we can see social networks being used to express and enable support for others as well. Technology has allowed ease of this value to emerge and be acted upon.

So whatever a person's chosen activities, more support will help them deal with the challenges that can arise. By developing with the support of another, people grow further and faster, and feel able to test out possibilities. It can also make it more fun.

To recap, if the coachee feels they have even a slight need to increase their development in any area, as coach you should begin to think which line of development they need to focus on to move on. For example, if someone is constantly running into financial difficulties, then their financial line needs extending; is lacking in confidence and self-esteem, then their emotional line needs development; is tackling a task which is technically too difficult for them, then their cognitive level needs developing to enable them to get a better 'grasp'; has an attitude that their own well-being is all that ever matters and people are reacting against this, then their moral development may need extending, and so on. In this session, if you choose, this can be used as an exercise to start bringing it all together. This is when things become more integral.

Four areas
As a Developmental Coach looking to support someone in creating the life they want, you will usually need to focus on four main areas. Applying a little of the content of the next session's 4 Quadrant model, there follows a condensed version of some of the lines of development that exist within these quadrants, i.e. body, mind, relationships and money. This model will support your

internal thinking when coaching because using it shows any areas in the coachee's life that are not being considered or developed. This is almost a minimalist model (in comparison to certain other areas of the book) but it should be viewed in terms of the appropriate support that can be given. These are the minimum conditions that need to be set up in life. Whether using the GROW model, or a life plan, this should give some guidance about to what to look for in a coachee's life and whether the conditions are accordingly set up. This session then is the start to thinking about the "spread" of a person's life activities. You may find yourself nudging them in some new directions of which they hadn't as yet thought.

Body

Good health is clearly an important element for almost, if not, everyone. But so often, and echoing the words of Carly Simon, we don't know what we have until its gone. Good diet, exercise such as gym or hatha (physical) yoga, physical activity such as walking, cycling and gardening are all aspects of good physical health. If a person is able to deal with a condition through medical treatment or alternative treatment they might, in the case of a back problem, find themselves considerably enhancing their life quality. For those without a physical focus, they may not initially see the benefits, but they will be felt soon after taking the appropriate actions. Dietary concerns are also paramount and a sensible eating regime certainly sets up the conditions for a healthy body.

Mind (and emotions)

They need to be thinking in a way and at a level that will aid their movement in life, as we discussed. Also, dealing with appropriate emotional responses, including the line of development called 'affect', as well as the adaptations and sub personalities all need to be considered. When a person is more emotionally balanced, their quality of life can generally be improved.

Relationships

A good approach to developing healthy and kind relationships is essential and this includes increasing the breadth of concern one has for all types of people. So often fulfilment in life will often come from our interactions with others. It can be lonely being successful when you don't have anyone to enjoy it with.

Financial

You may be surprised to hear that the fourth condition is money. You need to earn enough to allow you to have the activities you want in your life. In a Western society, working on this aspect of life will resolve many of the difficulties you experience. If you look at many of the problem areas in people's lives, how many of them are connected to money issues? At this point in 2012 when recession looms once more, this is truer than ever. When people work with this area of life, they set up the right conditions to do the work in many of the other ones. Also, in another way (and as we are seeing these areas as integral) if someone improves their emotional or relational abilities it is almost certain to have a positive impact on this fourth condition of money.

Clearly, knowing whether these conditions are set up will point you in the direction of the appropriate support for the coachee.

Successes and limitations

Over time Developmental Coaching can lead to deep and permanent transformations for the coachee. But it will come down to both the skill and approach of the coach, as well as the coachee and how they are 'put together'. Below I have brought together case studies from different areas, including the areas of health, relationships and business. As I am suggesting that all areas need to be seen as integral, I will attempt to make explicit certain key points as an aid to understanding how to apply what is written, but I would encourage your thinking to be far beyond 'as if', where you only take what I have written and apply it almost word for word to what you experience. Instead, explore the integral life that you and others are living – in this way you will begin to appreciate the applications of an Developmental Coaching approach.

Case study 1

Julia, a Buddhist meditation teacher in her mid forties, used an integral approach not just to solve a problem, but to move on as well.

Julia lived alone and committed many hours a week to her own silent sitting meditation practice. She ran open groups four days a week, in which she taught upwards of 10 people at a time. She rarely travelled except to leave the country for a group retreat once a year. In fact, Julia hardly ever left her neighbourhood. Her abilities within the confines of the teaching environment were considerable. Outside of that context she tended to have difficulties communicating in a way that people could relate to. She also had a tendency to look down on others and this resulted in her coming across as a little distant. She spent much of her time being 'calm'.

After several years of the same routine she had to deal with a serious health condition. Her energy levels had become particularly low and a problem developed with her digestive system. Throwing up many philosophical concerns around her meditation practice, she decided to seek support outside of her chosen school of Buddhism. Interestingly she had used the adaptation of reaction formation for many years – giving up alcohol, sex and tasty food, as this was required of her as a follower of the path of renunciation. When we met, I encouraged her to explore the four areas of life (Wilber's 4 Quadrants). As she talked through how she felt about her illness, it was clear that it had reached 'into her' at an identity level. 'Meditators aren't meant to get ill!' This attack on the self threatened who she considered to be 'I' (within the self system).

As a coach I supported Julia as she began to see that she had a choice of what to do next. Over a few conversations she began not to 'feel' so concerned at an identity level, but wanted to become well again. The decision was made to follow a route of exercise and hatha yoga was the preferred vehicle (the body being one of the four areas she had neglected), even though that was not within her Buddhist tradition.

A few months later, she decided to 'live a little' and stopped being so hard on herself. As a result, she began to loosen up and take a more healthily adaptive approach – she even let go of her non-drinking and had a humorous approach to an occasional drink. When she felt fully healthy once again, she taught meditation but with a higher degree of humour than ever before. Also the practice of yoga that she had undertaken herself became a recommendation to all her students – 'you can't ignore the body when exploring the mind'.

So Julia managed to move on from her 'neurotic adaptation' to one that was more connected to humour. She also extended her physiological line of development and began to operate with more balance across the 4 quadrants.

Case study 2

In another coaching situation, the coach aided the transition from 'what if?' thinking to more 'full what if?' thinking.

Rachel, an incredibly kind person, had spent five years nursing sick children in India before returning to her 'real life'. Even though she had seen some tough times, she was somewhat protected from life at home. She didn't have to earn any money, deal with family issues, progress in a 'career' and, especially, she didn't have to deal with her own emotional difficulties.

From a young age, Rachel was bullied at school for her freckles and goofy teeth. Though her physical appearance as an adult had become pretty, the emotional damage remained. She was obsessed about her appearance and utilised neurotic adaptations to protect herself. She was finding it difficult to handle situations that tested her – as she put it, she felt she wasn't as 'good' as the people around her. Despite her strong moral stance, she was lacking enough emotional development for her to both deal with her past issues and know that really she was more than 'good enough'.

Over the next year, spending more time with me as a coach (and a friend) allowed her to feel confident going for the jobs she wanted. The support provided aided her in reflecting on how she felt about herself. She was able to see through the old internalised image of herself and began to internalise the person she had become.

After a while she became a nurse in a casualty ward, dealing with the daily challenge of her patients' lack of patience. Soon, she didn't take her patients' irritability and impatience 'personally', and this transferred to other areas of life as well. She started to 'go for things' a little more. Personal confidence was a healthy balance alongside the concern she kept for others around her.

Case study 3

In a very different coaching situation, in this case I found it impossible to break through. This was a coachee who was utilising immature defences and failed to see other people's points of view. Their level of thinking remained as 'as if'.

It seemed that whenever Samuel snapped his fingers, people around him jumped. From an early age he was seen as the 'boss', but now aged 42, things should have changed.

At work he was always asking more and more of others, but giving less and less of himself – on the signature of an email he sent around it even read, 'If the people around me don't change, I change the people around me.' The world, he thought, revolved around him.

From a coaching perspective I was unable to adjust Samuel's thinking in the few sessions we had together. Quite simply, the depth of relationship was not enough to work at this level; nor was there any motivation for the coachee to do so. This case illustrates the limitations of coaching. The coachee does not see a problem and myself, as the coach, does not have the right to force a change. If, however, Samuel found his actions were no longer working (such as a high staff turnover due to his approach) then he might be prepared to look further at himself. The shift from 'as if' to 'what if' in this case would be the increase in understanding of other people's needs as well as their own.

Case study 4
In contrast, the next case study is interesting because a few coaching sessions of a different nature had quite major impacts on the coachee's whole life.

As a 13-year-old rebel, Tom was never keen on academic work and was never really encouraged to be. He was regularly provoking his colleagues and teachers and was becoming more difficult to control. His parents became more and more concerned yet did not know what to do.

A teacher took on an integral approach and saw that Tom had raw energy and was avoiding his competitive nature. As the teacher was also the coach of a local rugby team, one night he asked Tom to join the team in a rugby training session, a sport that was not taught at Tom's school. Tom, who was found it difficult to communicate with people different to himself, reluctantly agreed.

After the initial baptism of fire, being thrown into a mixed social group of varying ages, over many sessions Tom began to become more part of the rugby team. He continued to throw his weight around, but with his coach's help, he had at least started to direct his energies to sport. His schoolwork was not improved through this alone though.

Tom was used to being 'picked on' when he did things wrong – his teachers would punish him over and over for late homework, but to no avail. The teacher/coach spoke with a couple of the teachers about how much Tom responded to being encouraged, and they took this onboard. The next semester, two of Tom's teachers reported results which 'looked promising'. Tom began to feel people were helping his progress – he may also have felt a little proud about his own achievement, something that had never happened previously.

Tom had managed to move from the adaptation of passive aggression (and the overt acting out of the aggression) to one that was more mature. This also aided his transition to a higher level of being whereby be managed to make the move towards 'what if?' thinking through operating as part of a team. It was through this 'team player' role that allowed him to achieve at a suitably young age what Samuel in case study 3 was unable to do.

This coaching approach came from someone who may not have understood the theory of what Tom was going through and the adaptations he was employing, but this was unimportant in this situation. Tom needed someone to believe there was more to him than just his behaviours and it was through the medium of a team that he became more adjusted and well adapted. It actually aided him to 'come out of himself' and Tom could release the old immature defences as he became more appreciate of others.

Case study 5

In a similar vein, the last case study for this chapter shows how the support role can come in many different forms. In case study 5, the translations that the individuals explored failed and left them with the option to move on or move backwards. The result was that the relationship took on new meaning at a higher level; this transformed both of the individuals in that relationship to an extent that neither could have determined.

Tessa, a single parent aged 51, had done quite brilliantly to ride the roller coaster that was her life. Having found love in her later years only to have it taken from her through illness, she had begun to feel alone. Her children had left home and for a time their visits provided enough support to nurture her mothering needs. More recently though, her life had become too much to handle. Her youngest son Jim had left on his travels and rumours had been circulating that he may not return for another year. There was part of her that was desperate for the support and proximity of their relationship – the other part was willing to let him go. All the while her friends were telling her to 'snap out of it' and, without meaning to be cruel, they were certainly not helping.

When all was looking as though life had lost its meaning, Jim returned. After almost two years abroad and away from family, he returned to live in Tessa's home. Full of good ideas, the unlikely coach talked about life as he saw it, describing a rich tapestry of freedom and friendship. He tried to make his mother more positive and teach her things he had learnt. For several months he attempted to change her diet, her attitude, reintroduce key friends back in her life, while also getting her finances back in shape. His mother, although delighted to see him and have his support, she just wanted to hold him tight; 'her baby'.

Eventually Tessa's affections became too stifling, and since he was feeling he had failed, Jim began spending more and more time visiting friends. The support that Tessa so needed was unwittingly being withdrawn.

Soon after, Jim 'escaped' to the States for a while to study in a workshop. This avoidance worked quite well for the time, but he knew it wouldn't last. On his return, he sat in his mother's lounge and asked how she was feeling. Tessa looked down and began to say how alone she felt. Maybe due to jet lag but more likely something else, he began to cry. He said, 'I don't know what else I can do', as the tears began to stream. It was all the sadness that came from his efforts not working. On seeing this, Tessa ran from the other side of her room, crying. She placed her arms around Jim and she said, 'We will get through this.'

Within six months Tessa had created a fully independent life with more emotional wealth than she could have ever imagined. And why – simply because she knew once more the support and love of her son. His arm around her shoulder once in a while is what she desired most of all.

It was at this point of breakthrough that the relationship became something more encompassing than mother/son relationship. And it was at this point that all of the work to support her in her four life areas (body, mind and emotions, relationships and money) actually began to pay off. The unlikely coach was able to offer support in a most fundamental way, and it was when the relationship took on new meaning and new depths that the transformations in her life occurred.

Questions for reflection

Are your communications cleanly interpreted by the coachee?
Does your personal profile affect the coaching session?
Is there reciprocation in your coaching relationships? What relationship are you setting up?
When should you pass the supporting role to another expert?
What support do you have in your own life?
What will tell you whether the coachee is being over or under supported?

Session 7

4 Quadrant thinking

4 Quadrant thinking

I really appreciate Ken Wilber's work. His ongoing development of a framework enables so many people to understand the world better. As well as my formal studies in Organisational Psychology (University of London, Birkbeck College- an excellent programme) it has been superb to have the time to spend years studying his work. On a personal level, placing my own experiences into a larger developmental, or should I say integral, framework allowed a 'bringing together', through my own efforts and with much guidance from my own coaches, that I 'brought myself together.'

Years ago I used to enthusiastically begin discussing Wilber's work in great detail in the first session with a coachee. Over time, however, I have found myself sitting with a pen and paper, as I scribble through this incredibly useful model in a later session. For Devlopmental Coaching we will focus on the practical applications how you can use this with the coachee at this stage.I find you will achieve better results, as will with coachees, if you understand their areas of relative focus in relation to the model.

Let me now begin a scenario that this session will unpack as we go: What is necessary for me to understand the following phrase? 'I am a creative Developmental Coach'.

Here we have a question that could be answered in many different ways. From the use of 'I am...', we can all see that it is a statement about 'identity'. It also says something about how I see myself, i.e. 'creative'. For me to say I am creative may mean that factors other than my self-perception of 'me' as a practitioner are operating. Furthermore, for me to make any value judgement of my capabilities, there must be an interpretation of what I do within the coaching culture – I must have interpreted what I do and where I do it within the context of the coaching culture/community. In other words, I must be comparing myself. So the identity level statement is not just a comment about myself, but also says that I exist within the coaching culture. The statement of 'I' therefore has a relationship with 'We', i.e. the coaching community. Also, for me to be a coach, I might have received some sort of certification proving I am qualified, or my coaching qualification may be based on qualifications I already have – this may be from a university, professional body etc. There will have been a system in place that recognises me (or at least a system such as the business I operate in).

So, the statement exists in 4 domains:

mind – 'I' actually experience the thought in my mind

there are correlative changes in brain chemistry – 'it', e.g. synapses fire in the brain etc. It is also the realm of observable behaviour – I 'do' something as coach

culture – 'we', to agree or disagree with the statement

society – 'its' – society has processes for certification and application

In order to have a more complete understanding of reality at whatever level of consciousness, Wilber suggests that all four quadrants (I, we, it and its) need to be considered in all life areas. To ignore any one is to reduce 'reality' into something that it is not. In the coaching context, it may help to broaden the way a person thinks about their life and its workings. In fact, I think it is part of the fabric of this process. Makes sense?

Let's now start unpacking and expanding the 4 Quadrant model and its applications with an overview. We will then move on to relate its applications to coaching and Gallwey's GROW model.

The overview

Here comes another model for you to get on board. Hold on tight! In Ken Wilber's A Theory of Everything (one of many of Wilber's books to include this model), he explains that existence has developed through 4 distinct, but not separate, areas.

From the moment of the Big Bang at the beginning of time (shown symbolically in the centre), there has been an evolution in different areas. When humans came on the scene, it is expressed through the four areas of "I, we, it and its". They are manifested as: what is going on inside you (your thoughts, perceptions etc), your body (and brain), the society you live in and the culture (or shared view of the world).

The Individual quadrants

Before turning to the collective quadrants, let us look at the individual ones – 'I' and 'it'. The suggestion is that there is a direct correlation between the two quadrants, and that without the brain, there can be no mind. Think to yourself, 'I am going to read a coaching book'. You will have experienced the thought, 'I am going to read a coaching book'. The thought will have contained words or pictures, or both. There is also corresponding activity in the brain, i.e. brain-wave state changes, dopamine increases etc. And in this sense, 'I', at a fundamental level, do something – a behaviour – I read.

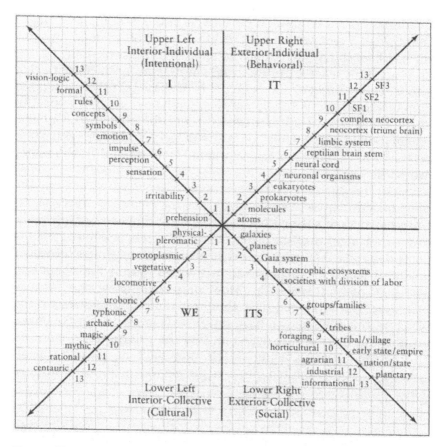

Ken Wilber's 4 Quadrant model

So what is the major difference between the brain and mind? As you know, the brain and behaviour are tangible 'things' that can be objectively observed but for mind, you have to ask questions or experience the content. No matter how much external prodding and poking around you do, you will not find the experience of the thought. The 'it' and 'its' quadrants are the realms of science and social science – and the tendency has been 'If you can't hit it with a hammer, it ain't real!' However, the thought *is* experienced. This is the 'I' domain – the inner world of experience – just as valid, but experienced internally. The 'it' or brain domain is not separate from the 'I' domain but, nonetheless, is different.

In much personal development we tend to focus on the upper left quadrant, i.e. we tend to be very much in the 'I' domain – 'what I think, what I feel, what I believe' etc. On the other hand, in some forms of coaching, there tends to be a focus on behaviour, i.e. the 'it' domain – 'what I can do'. And there is no problem with that either. The point of Wilber's model is to show that there are other domains to which 'I' and 'it' are firmly related and inseparable. In effect, the 'I' and 'it' cannot exist without the other two domains, but an individual can focus more attention in study and application on the 'I' or 'it' domains (as they could [and often do] with either 'we' or 'its').

The Collective areas

Imagine yourself sitting on a park bench and not seeing anyone – ever – nor at your office or bookshop. It is not possible, as life is dependent on other people. And so also is coaching. The lower left quadrant (culture) refers to values that we share with others at a particular point. It is also the "view" of the culture we exist within - this view has developed over time, but different cultures on the planet at this time all can have different views. The way we 'make meaning' of the world is dependant on the culture that we are in. The phrase 'Developmental Coach' may have no meaning at all outside of a quite limited circle of people; but within it there are many meanings bounding around, don't they? For instance, for Developmental Coaching it could mean that people have a shared view: this type of coach has studied some developmental psychology, has good interpersonal skills and are endeavouring to continue their own personal development.' In other words, there is mutual understanding within the culture.

Culture does, however, have its own 'it' correlate. This is the social system that culture exists within. For example, for the thought 'I am going to coach my colleagues at the office', there must be a system set up whereby a person can gain the appropriate coaching knowledge. There must also be no restrictions upon someone coaching, per se, or no restrictions on coaching at the office. So the social system is about rules, regulations etc. There is also the use of the technology that is available (a social system facet) e.g. skype chat, email, phone etc.

On the other hand, the culture will add meaning to this whole event. There is general consensus within the cultural worldview as to whether the event is worthwhile, good/bad and so on, i.e. culture adds 'meaning', interpretation or value to the event. For example, what do colleagues think when you go for a coaching session?

4 quadrant thinking and GROW

Bringing this model together with the goal setting approach from our very first session we will now look at a specific example. This will begin to show its importance within the coaching context. I bet you are feeling warm feeling now that we are tying it all together!

I regularly talk people through 'seeing the world with clearer, 4 quadrant lenses' and the results never cease to amaze me. In one instance I remember talking with a coachee who was having a 'personal crisis', having lost her belief in herself. I decided it was appropriate to explore this within the 4 quadrants of her life. Initially I didn't say that I was exploring 'her world' through the 4 Quadrant model, but I was. We explored how she thought and felt, how she was acting, who she was relating to and the business she was in. As there had been a new customer booking system introduced within her department, as a senior manager with responsibility for communicating the message of these changes she realised that the culture was rejecting the new processes and how this was causing her personal problems. When she saw that her feelings of failure were related to how the changes were being communicated, she felt free to take appropriate action (which, in this case involved a team meeting and action learning within the group). As I moved towards the close of the interaction she told me that her thinking was now somehow more 'complete' and more 'encompassing' than an hour earlier. The initial problem no longer felt the same. She felt she had been brought 'more together'.

On another occasion I worked with senior Fire and Rescue Service personnel to analyse the 2011 riots in London. We discussed how an individual's behaviour (it) was affected by their poor access to education and resultant attitudes (I) but how their communities (we) felt disenfranchised from the current social system (its). This is a sad and complex issue in cities where rich and poor live within minutes of one and other. The question became how best to intervene to a) prevent future incidents, but also b) to improve the situation for all parties. There will inevitably be multiple approaches to how best to solve such issues, including educational improvements and training opportunities, individuals' "feeling heard", community based projects, tax and benefits adjustments based on behaviours.

The journey through these four areas really is fundamental for coaching and I recommend you personally explore which of the lenses within your own 4 quadrant spectacles are clouded over, and which ones contain a stronger lens – I, we, it or its. When you strengthen all the lenses together, your world truly will look quite different; your world will actually change before your eyes – the world will change within your mind.

Let's look now at an example of using GROW before looking once again at the 4 Quadrants and then bringing them together. In the coaching context you may find that the coachee actually brings a straightforward and primarily behaviourally-based problem to you. If they say, 'I am not good at presentations', you may start to explore, using the GROW model, what they want instead. In this case you have begun with the Reality before the Goal – this is very common. If you establish what they want is 'To believe I can perform well in front of an audience', you have yourself the Goal. Next you may look at what the person can do about this, what are their Options? After a while they may decide that, out of all the possible options, they just need to believe they are able 'to learn how to perform better in front of an audience'. The final stage will be 'What next?'

To move from the Goal stage in this example to the Options stage, in particular, is quite a jump and one that many coaches would love to help their clients make even more quickly and effectively. Through understanding the 4 Quadrant approach, the coach can talk using language that respectfully engages the 4 Quadrants of the coachee's world. This, I am suggesting, will help the coachee not only make a change, but also aid their long-term development too.

Next, and on the same theme, let's take belief through the 4 Quadrants. When you say, 'I believe I am able to learn how to present better', the belief has expression within the four domains of body, mind, culture and society. Thus, 'I' experience the thought as a string of inner dialogue and some visual images. Again, the brain's dopamine levels will change, synapses fire etc – 'it'. If a different language was spoken, the belief would consist of different symbols or words with different meanings due to the culture – 'we'. Also, if there were no presentations to give, a different thought might be there. It may be, 'I'm going to enjoy ploughing the field.' – the social 'its'. So the thought is dependent upon other people (we) and the system (its) as well as the individual (I and its). Culture is necessary to develop these thoughts. If there were no people, who would the presentation be given to? Or, how can specific language develop without people to share it with? The same goes for the social quadrant. The level of technology (using this term to include agriculture etc) and existing codes of practice present determine the thought. Culture needs something substantial to operate in, e.g. buildings, technology, rules. The handouts from the presentation need to be printed and distributed; an overhead projector or computer are often needed.

The statement, 'I believe I am able to learn how to perform better', clearly needs all four quadrants to exist.

So, returning to the example and using GROW within the coaching session, the 4 Quadrant model could be used as follows:

'What would you be thinking and feeling if you did believe this?' – (I)

'How would your behaviours be different' – (It)

'What do your boss or colleagues think makes a good presenter?' – (We)

'How would this change the business system you operate in?' – (Its)

While they are being talked through the 4 Quadrants in this way, the coachee may reply:

'Well, I think I would feel more confident and know that I do most things very well.' – (I)

'I would spend more time preparing the overheads and slides that I will use.' – (It)

'There are people that I compare myself with that my boss considers good. And yes, I will talk with them about their approach.' – (We)

'Then, if I believe I can present well I know that it will affect the bottom line within my team. We will get more business.' – (Its)

You, as the coach, will have facilitated the coachee's world opening up to a more comprehensive way of thinking about their initial problem. They do something more than just shift the belief. Something will shift as the coachee, fundamentally, has worked out the problem for themselves within the complete four domains of life – I, we, it and its. Guidance on this occasion has been minimal, but it has been present throughout in the questions asked by the coach.

Making meaning

The Developmental Coach then is an integral coach as they understand that we all add a layer of interpretation to events. It is this interpretation that gives us our unique subjective, 'I', experience. We don't just experience life, we also interpret this experience – we 'make meaning' about life from this. When we, as individuals, look at an event, rarely will we all perceive (think and feel) the same way about it. The differences in the way we think and feel have a lot to do with the rich tapestry in human life. There are not many great artists that see what Picasso saw; nor are there enough world leaders that hold the vision for the planet in mind while acting on behalf of their nation. The world each of us think is the 'real' world is just the individual's version of the 'real world'.

This appreciation allows the coach to explore options that exist within the coachee's world. As I have indicated before, the coach should largely allow the coachee to hold the cards for the choices they make. Maybe the coach's role is, in part, to give the coachee a few more cards (or help them gain a few); or maybe it is for the coach to help the coachee take a leap so that the cards they hold become of a higher order. Whichever way, the coachee's (internal) cards will produce their view of the world and the coach should be careful to respectfully accept this view up to the point that it could cause harm to the coachee or someone else. Of course, if the coachee's view exceeded this point, then firm intervention is certainly valid. When you add the understanding of the nonseparateness/inter-dependence of culture and system, it becomes easier to understand that both the individual and collective domains have a relationship to meaning.

The Developmental Coach has the right to observe and comment on the coachee's haziness on any of the 4 Quadrant domains. If the coach notices that the coachee is focused, let's say, on how their colleagues feel (we), about what the coachee as an individual does (it), then the questions in the 'I' and 'its' domains will become important, i.e. because they are not being mentioned. Bringing out the 'I' and 'its' domains will lead to an expansion of view that will aid in the growth and development of the whole individual within the internal individual mind (I) and social (its) context. Remember that Developmental Coaching is not about fixing the problem alone (although this may be an element) – it is also potentially about growth and development through the solving of the problem. This is one of the reasons it is different to many other forms of coaching.

Some coaches may choose to explicitly show the 4 Quadrant model to the coachee at an earlier point in the journey, when the relationship has reached an appropriate stage, i.e. when they choose to be more explicit about the processes they use. Interestingly, this is when coaching begins to turn its naturally integral corner as it moves into a different frame. As the coach begins to take the coachee through such models as the 4 Quadrants explicitly, they begin to mentor (albeit at the earliest of stages). Mentoring allows for a higher level of guidance than conventional coaching. As I mentioned at the start, Developmental Coaching is not coaching alone. It will take on new meaning as the relationship between coach and coachee develops – a relationship, not surprisingly, that exists within 4 Quadrants. Whatever we do within the coaching context, it is learned and applied within the context of the 4 Quadrants. Understanding this, there can be more balance through developing mind, body, culture and social systems.

Re-balancing

This can be another way of approaching a coachee's goals and dreams, as well as their day-to-day activity. So, during this session

149

you want to be exploring this approach in as many ways as you possibly can.

It is because life exists within the 4 Quadrants that we need to realise the equal importance of each one and that they are non-separate/inter-dependent – they are integral. There is a tendency to over emphasise one of the Quadrant as being all-important, e.g. the Upper Left 'I'. But even though the functional locus of consciousness (mind) is the upper left quadrant, it is a distributed function across all 4 Quadrants. In other words, you cannot just develop any one quadrant without this leading to a distorted view. Within each of the Quadrants – mind (I), body and behaviour (It), culture (We) and society (Its) – there is a path of development and each Quadrant is affected by the development of another area. For example, in the social system (Its) Quadrant, the move into an Informational age will have seen a move that correlates to this in the cultural (We) Quadrant, an increase in the 'view' that is more 'world' than 'self' centred. But there will also be shifts in the other Quadrants as they are non-separate/inter-dependent. The individual will have new behaviours, e.g. social networking and potentially new ways of thinking that will help integrate all of the other parts. Think for a second how many changes in your personal networking have occurred since social networking sites have sprung up. Technology allows a new culture to emerge (or is the cultural need, first?) and we all think and behave differently to boot.

Things can go wrong!

There can be distortions that occur within any of the 4 Quadrants where development occurs. Even though we may see progress in some ways, we can be held back by the distortions of ineffective progress, just as we discussed earlier. Here are a few examples how they express themselves.

An individual can develop themselves to higher levels of thinking and being, but be held back by a lie they tell themselves, i.e. pushing out of consciousness an event they cannot face – this then affects their behaviours unconsciously. A person may have a condition such as dyslexia whereby their brain, in all other ways fully functioning, hasn't the required neurology to do a certain task. A culture could be brought together and founded in a religion that focused on devotion, but when the religion is distorted, it can

150

be a powerful weapon- 'if you kill on behalf of the religion, you will have life everlasting'. A society can say they are developing nuclear power as a safe form of energy when in fact, they have a distorted view in which the bi-products are used to make bombs. So, each domain therefore has its path and its distortions.

When an individual grows and develops ('I'), their personal view changes. However, unless the individual appreciates the necessary corresponding changes in all Quadrants, they will not see the changes needed in behavioural ('it') community service and cultural activities ('we'), techno-economic infrastructures and social systems ('its'). For an even more integral approach, the reader will need a thorough appreciation of all of the areas, as I have only touched on some Quadrants. In short, development of an individual manifests in all 4 Quadrants.

The main purpose of this 4 Quadrant model is the applications it has for human understanding of life. Without application it is interesting, but limited. As a result, finding points of application in business, education, medicine, politics etc are already well underway. Below I have suggested a sample of these applications. Please don't be limited by my own limitations of applications – both in here and out there, there is a 4 Quadrant world that is waiting for you to explore!

Health
With the frequent association that health exists in the 'I' and 'it' domains, it can be a coaching revelation to appreciate the cultural and social aspects to health as well. I have an example to illustrate this point, but before presenting it, I want to make the following point. I chose the example without any moral judgement and I hope with a little compassion to anyone whose circumstances are or have been similar. My intention is that the example will be an aid in applying and explaining the importance of this principle in terms of 4 Quadrant thinking, and to point towards a potential easing of such conditions. Sometimes you simply never know what your coaching sessions could involve...
Take as an example, if an individual has the misfortune to acquire a sexually transmitted disease. The 'it' domain would be the physical manifestation of the disease. The individual will usually receive a prescription from a doctor to deal with the physical

problem, but they may also 'feel' guilty about getting the disease – it may be through no fault of their own but, nonetheless, they feel the emotion of guilt. This guilt exists within the 'I' domain and is just as much an aspect to health as the physical realm. In turn, the individual may seek counselling to help with those negative feelings. They may also find that within their culture this condition is seen as a disgrace. Alternatively, their culture may accept that this is par for the course. Whichever way, the individual's feelings are likely to be affected by the culture they are part of – whether positively or negatively. This cultural consideration is in the 'we' domain. If the individual exists within a social structure that allows appropriate medicines to be supplied over the counter (a system question), then their feelings and condition may dissipate more quickly. If, however, the person could not afford the best treatment, then the body, mind and culture aspects will be affected. These are social system questions in the 'its' domain. Note: If alternatively the condition had been a facial skin complaint, it is observable how the individual can be affected in body, mind, culture (by people ignoring them etc) and social system (maybe the doctor's rules relating to priorities of treating or not treating skin complaints could become relevant).

This example proves how each of the domains impact on the person's health – it is not just about body; it is not even just about mind-body; it is about mind and body within the context of culture and society. Hopefully you have found that one useful to run through; as the coach, it is your role to support the understanding that health extends to all 4 domains of the Quadrant.

An interesting revelation that came out of one coaching session was that many health conditions improve considerably if you have money available to pay for the attendance of 'top' doctors. So 'its', in this case money, is a vital aspect of health. In the same way, diet (often related to both money and culture) also has an impact. To be healthy, we need then to apply our minds so that we appreciate how our health is embedded within each of the 4 Quadrants and that our health can actually develop to higher degrees through operating in these areas.

Here is another example when one coachee found he and his wife felt ('I') healthier not only when they did exercise ('its') but also when they socialised after their chosen sport ('We'). And of course the quality of social interactions are dependent upon the quality of that environment ('its'). See, I said there could be more fun using this approach.

Business

4 Quadrant thinking has already made its way into large corporate consultancies across the world. However, as 4 Quadrant thinking is only part of the larger integral framework this does not mean that the thinking is necessarily integral. Having said this, this model is still effective and relatively straightforward to grasp. One coachee who was running their own business found it fascinating that their mind had been fixed on the right hand domains ('it' and 'its') for so long that the left hand domains had suffered. The relationships ('we') can been neglected for many years (partly due to the internal challenges of the coachee). Quite simply, the relational aspects of business were, at best, ignored and, at worst, scoffed at. With staff turnover at an all time high, the business was finding that low morale on a cultural level ('we') was seriously affecting the behaviours within the roles ('it') and the bottom line of the business ('its'). It was only when a new senior manager who had the capability ('it') and attitude ('I') to develop long-term relationships that business began, slowly, to improve ('it'). A focus shifted to balancing out the 'its' with a new and transformed 'we'.

Business is not about systems; it is about systems related to the contexts of culture, behaviour and attitude etc. When any one domain ('I', 'we', 'it' or 'its') runs the show, there will be a detrimental effect. Another instance is that if the relational ('we') aspect alone is the only focus and systems are not kept up to date ('its'), then the business becomes less competitive if other businesses within the marketplace do keep up with the times.

Business success needs 4 Quadrant thinking and, if you analyse any successful business you know, they will have applied it – probably without actually knowing the theory.

Relationships

Taking a family situation, we can clearly see differences of culture ('we') between families – some families are at loggerheads while others have a culture of cooperation. Also, we can see how family relationships are impacted by social factors ('its'). For example, a family whose members have access to a good education ('its') may result in them becoming a family that sit around the table ('we') and discuss how they see world events. The individual behaviours ('it') that come from this will also be affected, e.g. their choice of job and opportunities are determined by individual competencies.

To show how 4 Quadrant thinking affects a relationship within a family, let's look at a problem faced by one coachee. The coachee's teenage son was going through a wayward phase of smoking pot and going on drinking binges. The main problem to stem from this was school truancy – he would not get up after she went to work herself.

She had tried to do everything to change his behaviour and had failed ('it').

She was left confused and frustrated ('I').

The family was also becoming affected as a whole ('we') as the son was not setting a good example to the younger children in the family.

After talking it through, the coachee began to see that her laissez faire attitude to child rearing may need to change. As family rules and regulations will affect any individual member's behaviours and feelings within the family, she decided to look at this quadrant as an area to change ('its'). Not wishing to stamp out personal freedom totally, she decided to 'do a deal' to charge her errant son a small rent out of his allowance for every day he failed to make it to school; and for every day he did make it, this money was doubled and saved on his behalf for his first car. This social shaping provided her son with enough personal motivation – the car – to get himself out of bed.

It was a 4 Quadrant result both for him and for her.

Now I bet you are already thinking about adaptations and levels of development in those last examples. Well, throughout the book we have used health, business and relationships as areas of application for Developmental Coaching. Now that we are coming to a close of this session, it is time to focus one more time on the importance of an integral approach within these areas. It is time to bring it all together. Whether this approach is through the Developmental Coaching relationship or through application by oneself, the affect is the same – an *integral* view and an *integral* approach leading to *integral* results. This approach should allow you to see more points of application when you are working with clients, chatting with colleagues or even observing your family and friends.

Integral health

Often we may think of 'the body getting ill', and in some cases this is true – there will be some kind of invasion of a virus, or maybe a cartilage wears down. But when it comes to health, as we saw in the 4 Quadrant example above, the role of many other factors must be taken into account, beyond just the body. Using it as an illustration, George Vaillant says, "when we lose someone whom we love, it is never the mind that is broken, only our heart, and feelings can mysteriously leap from the mind to the body." This connection of 'feelings' to health has its foundation in the upper quadrants of mind and body. The mind contains the feelings that we experience. It is through the reflective capacity of mind that the feelings are experienced. But because the feelings have a location in the body, there is a response in the physical body as well.

Bringing this together with the 4 quadrants, even though the physical 'Body' is an 'it', the experience of the subjective feelings, emotions and sensations of the 'body' are actual within the 'I' domain. So the 'Body' is objective whereas the 'body' is in the mind (a subjective experience). A point that is important to grasp as a Developmental Coach using the 4 Quadrants because it shows the importance of the correlation between mind and body/behaviour. The two are non separate; and in fact, the 'body' of the senses is included within the mind. As coach, this understanding will integrate your coaching approach in certain areas. Concerning health, it may be that feelings impact on physical well-being.

Healing the mind-body split

There is a very common phenomena you will probably come across in your own world- the body and the mind are often not integrated. To explain it this way, a person develops from 'being' just their body; at the earliest stage of development as a child, the child is their sensations and basic emotions etc. For Developmental Coaching purposes, this stage is pre-operational and due to its fundamental level, I have not focused on it – any problems that come from the child stage are usually not within the realm of coaching, but remember all the work you have done on adaptations as well. It is after this stage that the mind becomes more who they consider themselves to be. As with all evolution there is a movement away from the initial structure and onto a new, more complete one. This movement includes what went before it, but things can go wrong. If the stage before is shunned, like the major association with the body that existed until age 2, the individual will repress this part– they will turn against it and even 'cut' off contact. In this case, the part that is repressed is the feelings aspect of the body. If this happens, the body becomes separated from the mind. The body, as frequently happens, becomes separate and secondary, cut off from the sensations, emotions etc. This is very common and is alluded to when James Joyce said, "Mr Duffy lived a short distance from his body".

The body/mind split occurs for several reasons. The ego (simply meaning "I") sees that what stops its immortality is the inevitable demise of the body. Hence this is a very common defence. The ego believes it can live forever; the body, as the ego knows, cannot. So, the ego will dissociate, or split off, from the body. Frequently this continues until one of two things happens – the body either becomes ill, a situation that has to be dealt with, or the person transcends their ego level and goes beyond it, i.e. it re-members (reintegrates) the body with the mind. The result is a body-mind that is more complete than just a mind. The body can be remembered at any stage of the process (and in some cases it may have never been lost). In order for this to happen, the physiological line of development would be followed using one of many practices such as a sport, martial arts, yoga, cycling etc. This allows for embodiment of the mental realm to occur. In fact, irrespective of healing the mind-body split, unless an individual embodies their experience through physical activity, then their learning will be only partial. The mind-body requires activation beyond the neural activation of 'mind' alone in order for an individual to develop to greater levels of capacity. So keep an eye out for that one as well.

As has already been considered, health is not just to do with mind and body. For optimal health, the other quadrants must also be considered. If an individual moves to a location where the food distribution network (social – its) is not set up, it may have a serious impact on their quality of health as they cannot eat so well. In a similar situation, if someone joins a group whose members hold strong vegetarian beliefs, the individual could find this culture (we) impacting on their health if the only food available was wild bore. Hence, this cultural restriction has a strong affect. Integral health has to have all 4 quadrants as a base. The lines of development, e.g. physiological, and to what extent they are developed, i.e. to what level, is clearly relevant. At increasingly high levels of awareness the meaning of 'health' can be refined as well. To a yoga practitioner or sportsman, the experience of health is likely to be different to a layman.

Approaching health from a different angle, a person with more mature adaptations is in a better position to deal with any health issues that might arise. Even if ill health occurs, such an individual can adapt well to the condition and, let's say, anticipate consequences or suppress until it is time for action. Humour also helps the individual feel better about what they are facing (as can anticipation, another mature defence) – in turn this will aid the individual's mind and body to be in the best possible state. So health is partially to do with a disease that enters the body, such as a viral infection, *but is does not end there*. The dis-ease of a person also has a role to play. If the 'self' has an identity problem with the job they are doing and are struggling to hold themselves together, they will also 'feel' less than optimal – these are the feelings that can become embodied and in turn cause ill health.

Business (revisited)
Throughout the book we have looked at 4 quadrant applications in business, often without stating so explicitly. But what about 4 quadrants in the publicly funded services 'business'? Though this varies from country to country, it will still depict the challenges being faced. Many of your coachees will have an interest within the public sector arenas either directly (working in them or supplying them with services) or indirectly as a citizen (as a recipient of services such as health, taxation or government). It is down to the reader to find their own applications and maybe even the occasional volunteer as coachee who will explore how this type of thinking is helpful to them. There are many people in business who are more than happy to receive support on issues they are currently facing- coaching and consulting businesses continue to thrive as the pace of change within organisations continues to speed up.

On a personal note, on one occasion my coach called me when I was working on a business consulting project and asked how things were going. I explained I had talked someone through the 4 quadrant model and, though this Director usually challenged any new ideas, they ran with it and were talking about restructuring because they 'now see more clearly'. They then made a radical decision to integrate their internal communication system so that the culture of the organisation would feel included in all of their product and service areas (as opposed to departmentalism). Also, individuals would be financially rewarded according to their contribution to the success of the entire organisation. I explained to my coach that I was slightly shocked at how large a change had come about when I expected the Director to pick holes in it. 'Why?' he inquired. My coach then said something that I like, 'What else could they say? The model is robust.' Looking at its applications, I hope you too can see the scope that an integral approach has and how robust it truly is.

On another occasion, a Director of a small private company once said, 'Too much demand. What a great problem to have!' He saw that his company would achieve its targets by increasing the efficiency of the staff, improving the way the workforce felt about their work, sharing the rewards of increased profits with all employees and paying for new equipment if needed. With less than 50 employees, his 4 quadrant actions were able to support the business's growth and development. But in the public sector, too much demand over-stretches available resources and the key resource is the people providing the service. The fact that any government-funded system must be rationed leads to an automatic problem – the allocated funds must be distributed as fairly as possible for the interest of all parties, and when they run out, they run out. (well, supposedly but have you seen those deficit figures?!) This contributes to the psychological conflict that 'We want to do more, but can't' (upper quadrants). It is not just to do with money either. This can be seen, let's say, in the police service where an officer wants to be in active service, but needs to fulfil bureaucratic requirements; or a teacher who spends more time dealing with 'organisational' issues than they do teaching. In the private sector, more often than not, a director is looking for a return on capital. But the public sector is often constrained by the politics of the day – and politics vary with whichever political party is in power. Success in the public sector is showcased, while failing public services are named and shamed for all to see. This significantly affects the public services' cultural psychology as employees are caught between doing a good job for the 'customer' and satisfying the holders of the purse strings too. However while the system creates many of its own problems, it may also be the basis of their solution. But changing the system in a huge business (private or public) is not easy, illustrated by the adage that goes 'if you take a lousy system and you make it more efficient, what do you get? ...A more efficiently lousy system!' This could be further illustrated by someone attempting to make the paper-based patient's records system more effective by filing them differently – in contrast, some foreign health services use hand held computers to log patient information instead of using paper records. So even though changing the system is a challenge, maybe it is a challenge worth taking.

It is those who can transcend the current view of a system and see it from the outside that make the most effective long-term changes. It is those who can create the systems, instead of adapting to them, that will move the 'business' on. Individuals who can see possibilities beyond the current level of culture and systems can implement changes in that system when the opportunity, i.e. new money or a new initiative, arises. There is also an impact on shared culture and individuals' attitudes and behaviours. For instance, a doctor working in both the public and private sectors may not have the resources to operate in their chosen way in their public sector work, while they can do so in the private sector. When the opportunity arises, they can operate at the higher level of treatment, or thinking, in the public sector as well. Their behaviour and attitudes change as they are freed up to do what they consider to be a better service. Whether we are talking about education, health or local and police authorities the principles will stand because all such services are, to a large extent, constrained by the system.

This last section has been a tour around the 4 quadrants with recognition that if any one quadrant is changed, there will be an impact on the others. And it is not something that stands still. This is a dynamic process that needs monitoring with the necessary interventions at the right time. From a business perspective, acting within all 4 quadrants, looking at attitude, behaviour, culture and systems, is a more complete approach to management than choosing either what is 'in vogue', or one's own preferences.
For your coaching sessions, the 4 quadrants have instant applications in the business world, but there are also the other

elements such as levels of development. Just as we spoke of 'as if', 'what if?', 'full what if?' and 'what what if?' as levels of consciousness, there are also levels that exist within business. These have their correlates in the lower left quadrant of culture too. There is a movement from a social system that supports 'dog eat dog' culture through to ones that enable all individuals to express more compassion and understanding. An illustration would be a business that encouraged salesmen to work just for themselves. Or at a higher level, for themselves and their team. Or at an even higher level for themselves, their team and the good of the community – and in return gain greater rewards at each higher level. And the system can be, and needs to be, set up to allow this to occur. It is a case of looking at what level the system is currently at and how this supports the level of culture that is jointly experienced. From there the system and culture can be moved on. Frequently key individuals drive this change so the level of being they are operating at is vital to the whole process.

Integral relationships
Writer Paul Watzlawick says, "We all know what it means when one thing depends on another. But when the other thing depends on the first to an equal degree, so that they unavoidably influence each other, they are said to be interdependent.' Similarly, integral relationships are founded in reciprocity – this is not just two people who are independent of one another, but rather two people who are inexplicitly bound by the relationship themselves. In fact the relationship creates the person as much as the person creates the relationship. This is looking at relationships at a high level of where, as Kegan says in relation to conflict, "the parties can recognise each other's needs, views and fears, and consider solutions which reassure the other that their precious interests will be respected."

The level at which the relationship exists depends on the levels of consciousness of the parties involved. Aim to understand the level at which the parties are operating and support growth, instead of condemning them. From early on I have suggested that Developmental Coaching is a vehicle for the individuals to be changed by their relationship. Whether it is a coaching relationship, a business partnership, intimacy, family or friends, an integral relationship is based on appreciation of the other party, i.e. understanding their views, not trying to change who they are, but trying to engage with them in a way that allows the relationship to create new ways of being for all parties involved in the exchange. In relationships it is when there is reciprocity of feelings, of cognition and of language that individuals feel connected and integral. Concerning intimacy, this type of relationship transcends the lower levels where mere base desires are the binding force. This is not even just about emotions and having strong 'feelings' for another person. Instead this extends to how the individuals think and how they exchange those thoughts with each other, and then their extension of them back into their actions. When individuals have commonality at the higher levels, the exchanges not only create the relationship but also the form of the people within that relationship. This can then be extended out as a way of being to a wider culture of family and beyond. It can also be taken into the system area of life where an individual relates to others in a way that allows for the development of themselves and of the other party.

As an individual develops to a higher level of being (from 'as if' through to 'what what if?'), they will not 'lift up their anchor' and drift away from others. Instead in an integral sense they will find themselves more inclusive in their approach. With the sub-personalities integrated into a higher level order and the adaptations at a level that allows for more mature responses, they find themselves relating more at the level of another, not more beyond it. For the coach in particular it is worthwhile remembering that 'no one cares how much you know until they know how much you care'.

So, there we have it. The end of session seven. I truly hope that running through example after example has helped you to know how to apply these models. I have also aimed for you to see how the earlier sessions can be fitted together. The truth is, you will find your own way as a Developmental Coach. You might decide to call yourself an Integral Coach but, as I said from the start, you may well need to be reaching to the highest levels of human potential to truly be such a coach. You may well also need to consider areas I have missed as well, but we haven't done badly working together throughout this book to look at what it means to develop an individual.

Questions for reflection

In which Quadrants can you develop further as a coach?

Think of certain coachees. In which Quadrants can you support them to develop further?

Do you have a map of how they see the world? Are there any areas of distortion you can help with?

How will you now approach your coaching sessions differently?

Are coachees aware of the mind-body continuum? Do they maintain good health? Are they prone to frequent but mild illness?

Do coachees, of whatever type, understand the role of the 4 quadrants in their business life?

Are the coachees engaging in reciprocal relationships with those around them? If not, how will you help them?

Conclusion

I would like to end the book where I started, but maybe now we can re-enter at a higher level now we understand each other better. Developmental Coaching is rooted in Integral Psychology, including the work of Ken Wilber, Robert Kegan, George Vaillant, David Kolb and Carl Rogers. But when it is combined with the vehicle of coaching it becomes a way for an individual to support the development of another human being. It is the ability to support the increase of personal competencies; support the emergence of the next stage of consciousness; assist in rejecting lower stage adaptations in favour of those that are more mature; it is action across several developmental lines; it is motion within the 4 quadrants of life; it is a thorough embrace of one's dreams and aspirations as the self goes on its journey. Developmental Coaching is about living a good life, whatever that may mean for you. Even when there is no coach, there can still be the essence of an integral approach as all of these session can be applied to yourself.

When I work with a new client I tend to put together a package based on the sessions I have outlined. Sometimes they may have an interest in meditation, so I might teach the foundational skills in this area as I have been a practitioner for 16 years; they might be curious about their energy (chi/prana) so, as I was a Chi Kung (Chinese Yoga) Instructor many moons ago I may introduce some exercises where they experience this energy flow for themselves; if they really want to focus on the subtleties of communication, I may go back into my NLP training (as I am a Master Practitioner and Trainer); I may even dig out some of the research from my Organisational Psychology Post Grad studies and bring that to the table; I have also travelled and worked all over the world with individuals and in businesses. Most of the time, however, I aim to work within this central framework and treat everything else as supplementary. You get the idea though, just be yourself and allow the coachee's needs to determine the way the sessions progress. You already have tremendous life experience to draw from, so please don't be restricted or see the seven sessions as a formula. This is coaching that extends to the awakening, within every individual, the potential that they have. It is movement towards the highest reaches of what is means to be human, while keeping one's feet firmly on the ground. Your job is to help that process.

Developmental Coaching has covered several application areas including health, business and relationships. Aside from these three application areas I have focused on, I have also offered something that is perhaps of a more personal nature through the examples used. I usually point out this is not 'therapy', but seeing that we have entered at a higher level now, we might consider that it actually is a form of therapy – 'a macro therapy'. Not a therapy that aims to resolve a specific psychological or physical problem (nor a type of management approach that looks to resolve a specific business issue), but a therapy that allows for an individual to find their healthiest adaptation to life. Using the word 'therapy' loosely, we see that Developmental Coaching is about the growth and development of an individual through life and through all that could hold them back.

The coach themselves might be the first person on this journey and this is where I will leave you for now. It will be those that feel the burning desire to become this Developmental Coach that will follow the path. So where will you find such a coach to support you? If you follow the book suggestions below you will already have some of the best company for your journey.

I would like to end with a passage from Carl Roger in *On becoming a person.*:
"*If I can create a relationship characterised on my part:*
by a genuineness and transparency, in which I am my real feelings;
by a warm accepting of and prizing of the other person as a separate individual;
by a sensitive ability to see his world and himself as he sees them;
Then the other individual in the relationship:
will experience and understand aspects of himself which previously he repressed;
will find himself becoming better integrated, more able to function effectively;
will become more similar to the person he would like to be;
will be more self-directing and self-confident;
will become more of a person, more unique and more self-expressive;
will be more understanding and accepting of others;

166

will be able to cope with the problems of life more adequately and comfortably.
I believe that this statement holds whether I am speaking with a client, with a group of students or staff member, with my family or children."

It seems as though this statement can be extended into the coaching relationship. It is the essence of Developmental Coaching as well.

Recommended reading
Ken Wilber: 'A Theory of Everything'; 'Integral Psychology', 'Brief History of Everything', 'Integral Spirituality'.

When people ask where to begin with Ken Wilber's work, it is tempting to suggest a similar path to the one I have been following. If one starts at the beginning and works through to the present, the reader will enjoy the evolution of Ken Wilber's own work. As he expresses himself, there is a movement from the early models, eg Wilber I, that he adopted to ones that have gone beyond them, ie Wilber IV, often adjusting previous views as he himself develops. Many may find his later work (included in the books above) most relevant within the contexts included within this book. It will depend on time (which is really used as an excuse when we mean 'priority'), emerging passion (which is a sense that it is worthwhile) and, most of all, points of application available, as to how much of Wilber's work you take on board. I would encourage conversations around and about the texts as this truly helps to embody in actuality the meaning of the words that are written.

Robert Kegan: 'The Evolving Self'; 'In over our heads'
To sum up these two books, you have to comment on Robert Kegan himself. The content relating to holding environment and developmental progressions is excellent but you are also left with a sense that Robert Kegan is a kind man.

These books are an asset alongside other texts, such as Wilber, as they truly help the application of many developmental principles. As reader, you are drawn in to many people's lives as he explains how they express the joys and pains of developing, and not developing. It is especially useful in getting to grips with the intricacies of each stage and what is indicative of, for example, *the movement between 'what if?' and 'full what if?' stages of development.*

Carl Rogers: 'On becoming a person'
Carl Rogers also comes across as a kind man. Working for many years as a therapist, he has been the midwife to new personalities and this book is a testament to his patience and high level of concern for others. For the reader it will help them to appreciate their role as a coach and how to relate in the best manner for the optimum experience of the coachee. I recommend it highly.

Beck and Cowan: 'Spiral Dynamics'
Don Beck and Chris Cowan have done a wonderful thing. This book shows the movement through the levels of consciousness and the associated 'values' (similar to the moral line of development) that are indicative at each stage. The colour coding is soon picked up and becomes a useful language explaining, for instance, how the Integral individual at a 'yellow+' stage of development can relate to the whole spiral of other colours. The penetration of this model in the world has been astonishing and it is essential reading for any coach. While Ken Wilber gives overviews in his later books, the original text helps to further the reader's understanding by enjoyable and frequently very modern examples of people, countries and companies that are operating at the various stages of development.

George Vaillant: 'Adaptation to Life'
This book is probably best read after a framework has been built through reading Wilber and Kegan. It helps the reader find in themselves the adaptations they tend to employ through reading how people on the Grant Study have grown and developed through life. This book is truly a remarkable read unlike anything else, but a word of caution – it may be something not to share with others (particularly loved ones) as it will reveal to you enormous amounts about the ways we hold ourselves together. I would recommend seeing it as a mirror to your own soul for quite some time before turning the illumination towards others.

David Kolb: 'Experiential Learning'

This is a foundational book on how we learn through experience. It is superbly written and the reader is left with a deeper understanding into the meaning of 'integral' and 'integrated' which will help in coaching and in one's own development.

Sternberg and Kolligian: 'Competence Considered'
As a collection of essays on competence, the reader gathers a picture of the role of mind, body and behaviour, culture and social system in relation to competence. It is not a book focused on training certain skills, but more a book on the fundamental thinking required when it comes to skill transfer and attainment.

Howard Gardner: 'Multiple Intelligences' 'Frames of mind'
Gardner has opened up the view of 'intelligence' through his work. Highly acclaimed, these books increase one's own understanding of developmental lines and capabilities which will aid an integral approach.

Daniel Goleman: 'Meditative mind'
In the realm of human development, meditation has been under-explored as one of the key mechanisms for accelerating movements through the levels of consciousness. This book gives an overview of the processes to engage in personal practice. Even though meditation in 'mainstream' culture remains relatively small, it is through the clarity and demystification of the processes that people will see its direct and tangible benefits. For the integral self, it is a recommended practice that can be grounded in everyday living.

Michael Basseches: 'Dialectical thinking and adult development'
For the reader who has grasped much of the other material, this book gives an overview of the cognitive abilities of someone at the 'what what if?' stage (dialectical). It runs through twenty-four 'patterned movements in thought' that are characteristic of this level of thinking and being. It is quite technical in nature, beautifully written and a text to be referred to time and time again. Each time it seems to take on new meaning.

Roger Whitmore: 'Coaching for Performance'
This is an asset for all coaches looking to pull on an expert coach's experience. John Whitmore is an inspiration in this field. This book includes coaching techniques that are easy to apply in all areas of life and as it is written in a friendly style and with a clear layout, it is an excellent reference for any coach.

John Seymour and Joseph O'Connor: 'Introducing NLP'
This remains a wonderful introduction to NLP. Highly recommended for anyone looking to learn more about communication and self-mastery skills. I worked with John for ten years and he remains one of the best trainers in the world as well, so check out his courses too.

Tatiana Bachkirova: 'Developmental Coaching: working with the self'
This is a great book with a similar view of human development to my own. I haven't tried to integrate the principles as I would suggest you simply compare and contrast for yourself. The author has an excellent academic pedigree and utilises research to support the principles.

Otto E. Laske, PhD PsyD M.Ed: 'An Integrated Model of Developmental Coaching™: Researching New Ways of Coaching and Coach Education'
This is a brief online paper that is well worth reading! It utilises Kegan's work (and others) in a very solid, research based fashion.

Paul Ekman: 'Emotions Revealed' and 'Telling lies'
These are both excellent books on micro-expressions and how we "leak" our inner world outwards. Alongside skills for utilising what you see, this is a lovely resource to understand how to communicate even more effectively.

Testimonials:

"I have worked with Martin for many years and have experienced at first hand his rare combination of high level integrity, compassion and intellect. He has an exceptional ability to make a difference in peoples lives, and has done so repeatedly. If you are looking for a first class life coach, I can recommend Martin wholeheartedly."

John Seymour, NLP trainer, consultant and author

"Martin's phone coaching sessions really helped me to get focussed and clear about issues and goals both in my work and in my life generally. The weekly sessions helped me to reframe my thinking during a particularly difficult and hectic phase when I didn't have much time to travel to meetings. Martin has a great ability to move fluidly between the micro and the macro elements of an issue, providing connections and insights that continue to be really helpful."

Sally Angel, TV producer

"Martin Shervington is a creative genius & one of the most gifted & intelligent people I have known. His wit, insight & objectivity, combined with his selfless humility separate him from the ordinary, & while he possesses multiple talents, I am continually amazed & in awe of his ability in coaching sessions to use humor to turn the trivial into the sublime."

Bill Shewey, National Sales Director, Future US

"As a business man of some 20 years, it was my pleasure to attend personal management coaching sessions with Martin Shervington recently. The concept of the training was remarkably adaptable and certainly simple to follow, however it was Martins honest understanding of not only the subject matter but more importantly for myself. Having attended countless training and development training programs over the years it was refreshing to experience his measured approach and intelligent analysis of my strengths and areas for further development this made it the most influential training session I have attended in my career to date. I would have no hesitation in working with him again and was more than happy to pass his details to my associates, who I understand, have also been the recipients of his genuine approach and skills."

Simon Davies, Sales Director K2 Moving

"For over 25 years I have led and managed people but something was lacking and stalling my ability to advance on my professional vision, I so wish that somebody would have introduced me to Martin Shervington when I was setting out. Martin brings together a remarkably rich set of skills; personal entrepreneurial and executive experiences, keen insights into human development processes, an intuitive skill in identifying roadblocks and an ability to teach a wide range of tools for self analysis and self development. The results were very powerful. The insight I've received has really helped provide clarity in my mind about what I needed to do in a number of key situations. I have developed the tools and the know-how to effectively deal with even the most challenging situations. My drive and confidence have grown significantly providing much more satisfaction in my life and feeling better connected to my inner values and loving myself for who I really am. I recommend Martin Shervington's services to anyone who has a vision for their future and needs a boost. I assure you, like myself, you will grow and achieve through this experience in ways you didn't imagine and move towards impacting people in the way that you desire."

Mick Dixon, Strategic Manager – Avon Fire and Rescue Service

Get in touch:

Martin is available for coaching, training and consultancy all over world. He has considerable experience and knowledge in public sector, corporate and high pressured start-ups (especially tech).

He can help with:

One-to-one coaching

Project based consultancy

Facilitation and training

Executive brainstorming sessions

Developmental Coaching – 7 sessions

Executive coaching and solution focused sessions

His website is: www.martinshervington.com

Also find him on Linked and Facebook and Google+

Also From MX Publishing

Leadership and Entrepreurs Books

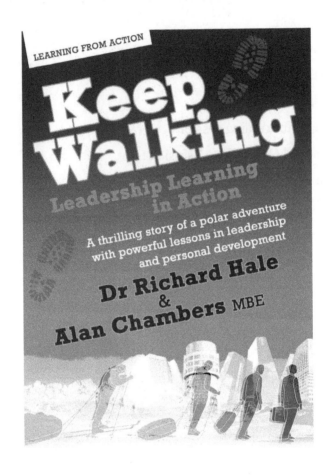

www.mxpublishing.co.uk

Also From MX Publishing

Leadership and Entrepreurs Books

www.mxpublishing.co.uk

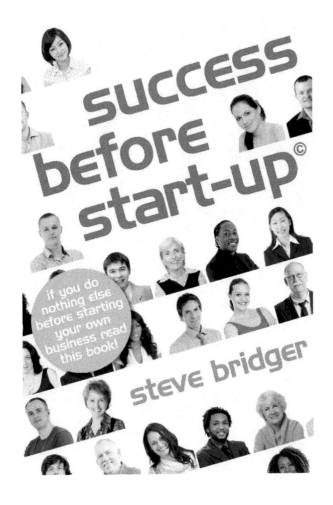

Lightning Source UK Ltd.
Milton Keynes UK
UKHW020953081219
354991UK00015B/582/P